PINHOE AS USED TO WAS

Also available in this series:

PINHOE AS USED TO WAS

Denys Deere-Jones

ISIS
LARGE PRINT
Oxford and Orlando

First published in Great Britain 2000
by Tabb House

Published in Large Print 2002 by ISIS Publishing Ltd,
7 Centremead, Osney Mead, Oxford OX2 0ES
by arrangement with Tabb House

British Library Cataloguing in Publication Data
Deere-Jones, Denys
  Pinhoe as used to was. - Large print ed.
  1.Deere-Jones, Denys - Childhood and youth 2.Large type
books 3.Pinhoe (England) - History - 20th century
4. Pinhoe (England) - Social life and customs - 20th century
I.Title
942.3'56'083'092

ISBN 0-7531-9776-6 (hb)
ISBN 0-7531-9777-4 (pb)

Printed and bound by Antony Rowe, Chippenham

FOREWORD

IN compiling this little book of reminiscences I have relied mostly on personal recollections and youthful impressions. Except in the interests of accuracy I have tried not to draw too freely on parish and county records, which would have meant a kind of cheating, although I have picked the brains of the curators of Exeter's Royal Albert Memorial Museum and the staff of the Devon Survey Office on one or two points, to whom I am grateful. In a few other instances, mainly references to people and events only remotely connected with Pinhoe: Poltimore, Killerton, the Fawcett Expedition, etc., I have borrowed from *The Acland Family* by Anne Acland and *Exploration Fawcett* edited by Colonel Fawcett's younger son Brian, my indebtedness to both of whom I freely acknowledge; also *Eighteenth Century Exeter* by Dr R. Newton, and *History of Exeter* by Professor W.G. Hoskins (a contemporary of my sister Marjorie at UCSW and occasional visitor at Westleigh during my childhood.)

With the exception of recent snippets of information from Pinhoe's long-serving Postmistress Miss Betty Cottrell, and Mrs Jean Hext formerly of Red Hayes, nearly everything else is put down from memory, including what I was told at the time by my elders and betters. For any errors in date or fact I and my memory must therefore by given the blame.

Littlecombe Shute, Branscombe
and Cullompton, 1999

CONTENTS

INTRODUCTION

Pinhoe, to my way of thinking, in those far-off days had never been much of a village. The Pin or Pinn Brook on which its original settlement had grown is now and presumably was then a mere three-mile short trickle. It was sufficient to run a mill, but only one, and not until a few thousand years after the village was founded, and then almost right up at its source with an artificial dam to give it sufficient head.

The Danes had a few goes at Pinhoe but only in passing, and out of spite as it were, because Exeter had kept them out; on one occasion at least they got the worst of it. Even in the heyday of its mediaeval and manorial well-being it may have suffered from too close proximity to its great historic neighbour, being nearly as close as those other once separate communities, Alphington, Exwick, Heavitree, Wonford, and even Whipton. These, by the start of the twentieth century, had already paid the penalty of being within the grasp of an insatiable civic monster, and become indistinguishable from each other with their rows of pretentious villas, less pretentious artisan terraces and all the paraphernalia of brickwork, glasswork, concrete work and roadwork resulting from unstoppable population growth and ceaseless commercial change. Pinhoe's additional two miles' distance made a difference, until recently.

Be that as it may, the Pinhoe of a 1920s childhood was still a village. It was separated from Exeter's eastern boundaries at neighbouring Whipton by quite a few measurable acres of woodland and grassland; from Stoke Canon over the hills by several miles of peaceful lanes, past the then unspoilt natural nature reserves of Huxham Brake, Stoke Hill and Stoke Woods; and from Heavitree by a formidable length of the Honiton and London Road. Along the leafy borders of this road and over the marshlands around the adjoining Moor Lane any number of wild birds proliferated and nested and sang, and as for a fast road, if after venturing along the road you chanced to encounter a *motor* car you ran all the way home breathless to tell every one about it.

The whole Moor Lane area is now an Industrial Estate.

There seems to be some doubt as to the derivation of the name Pinhoe. Early versions range from Pennoc and Peonha to Pynoo, none of which, taking into account changing fashions in phonetic spelling, local mispronunciations and indifferent copying from illegible manuscripts, are of much help. *Pen* rather than *Pin* may represent the Celtic term for head or hill, and the *oo* or *hoe* may be cognate with the village of Hooe on the south side of the Cattlewater opposite Plymouth, or even with the latter's famous water frontage.

There exists, however, a tiny stream, the Pinn Brook; though which came first, its name or that of the settlement on its banks, is a matter for further conjecture. The brook could hardly have been named from a topographical head or hill since it rises in the crutch of a *combe* or *clieve*. *Pen* of course also signifies an enclosure or pound for straying cattle, and Pinhoe used to have one of those. Its third meaning of "female swan" is surely not to be seriously considered here, in view of the brook's very modest dimensions, although within living memory its lower reaches provided shelter and sustenance to quite a few kingfishers, grebes, water rails and moorhens.

We are left with its alternative and present day spelling, *Pin* or *Pinn*. A pin-horse was the middle of a team of three. A *pin* also meant, and still means, a peg or a feather (pinion) besides its more commonplace association with needle — all obvious irrelevancies in this context. With a double "n" it suggests combination with a second syllable, as in Pinnoc — surely a mistransliteration (*c*. AD 100), or Pinnow (1400).

This *hoe* or *ow* or *how*, all three to be pronounced as in the bow of bow-and-arrows with a silent aspirate typical, as it still is today, of dialects other than those of the Westcountry, has to remain something of an enigma. A *hoe* among other things was as at Plymouth, "an outhrust ledge or heel of land overlooking or intruding upon an area of lower land or a stretch of water". Search as one may, there seems to be no such geographical feature around Pinhoe, nor for that matter at those other *hoes* elsewhere in the country: Caddihoe, Trentishoe, Morthoe, etc. *How* on the other hand, cognate with old Teutonic (Saxon) *haugh* meaning high, denotes a hill or hillock, sometimes a *tum* or *tummorth*, of which there are several in all those neighbourhoods.

On huygi hoo fram Escansis aest pen broc abof — as the Anglo-Saxon Chronicle might almost have put it.

Pinnow, Pinnor, Pinhow or Pinhoe, then; "Hill-above-the-Pinn". In fact, there is a hill on each side of the little Pinn Brook.

Well over three quarters of a century this writer's memories go back; not even a faint line on the human time-scale, yet a long way on from the AD 100s and 1400s. Yet the changes that have come about since the early part of this century, not only in and around Pinhoe, are such that today we live in a totally different world from that of seventy years ago, and Pinhoe has become no more than a village that "used to was".

Opinions vary as to whether the new world is so very much better, or whether the person responsible for the following pages and the little pencil sketches in them has changed for the better over the years. It is thanks to his fond mother that those early artistic efforts exist at all, though opinions may vary there, too, as to whether to be grateful.

CHAPTER
ONE

Early Days

In those days, in the 1920s, young Denys, usually known as Denny, lived with the rest of his family at Westleigh, halfway down Station Road. The station at the bottom is still there on the Exeter-Waterloo line, but for various reasons is no longer the station it was. His father, Mr Fred Jones, had been headmaster of the village Elementary (Church) School since 1912 (before Denny was born), except for war-time service with the Devonshire Regiment.

Westleigh was one of several properties in the village owned by Mr John Finning, who lived next door to it with his cook-housekeeper, Miss Dash. John Finning had been a widower for a number of years and his only son, Leonard, to whom Miss Dash had been engaged to be married, had been killed in that same War. A convenient arrangement for Mr Finning and Miss Dash had been reached, but with implications that drew frequent disapproving comments by John Finning's nearest neighbour and tenant, confided in private to his wife, often in Denny's puzzled presence. But Mr Finning was one of the managers of Pinhoe School so that its headmaster dared not air his prejudices too widely.

Denny had an older brother and sister, Howard and Marjorie. Howard went to a boarding-school at

Ashburton, some miles the other side of Haldon, and his sister to St Hilda's at Exeter. Marjorie showed some talent at the piano, eventually becoming a Licentiate of the Royal Academy of Music and a full-time teacher. Neither her elder nor younger brother showed comparable promise.

Bessie Joslyn, who lived only three or four doors away, was almost another member of the household. She could only have been about fourteen when she left Pinhoe School and took up her job at Westleigh. Bessie was ginger-haired and heavily freckled, and provided with a heart of gold. Her work at the house ranged between emptying the "charlies" that lived under the beds, cleaning out and relaying the fires in drawing-room and dining-room, helping in kitchen and scullery, and between times acting as the young boy's nursemaid.

These last duties often took the pair of them up Station Road and along the main road past the school, down Pinn Hill, past West Clyst Cottages and the tall rook-haunted elms of Moon Hill Copse, to Poltimore Park a mile or so east of the village, to look at the fallow deer and the red squirrels and in the autumn to pick up conkers. A journey on foot along that route today would be unpleasant and hazardous, past innumerable parked vehicles and being passed by innumerable un-parked ones, with no deer and certainly no red squirrels or conkers at the end of it. True, the ball-topped granite gate-posts at the entrance to what remains of the Park have been preserved, but the wooded sand-quarries on each side have been done away with.

2

In one of those quarries in the 1800s, and until recently on display in Exeter's Royal Albert Memorial Museum, a slab of sandstone with the toeprints of the mammalian reptile cynognathus had been discovered; evidence of a primaeval setting very different from the racing and racketing road-jungle there today.

During the earliest visits by Bessie and her young charge to Poltimore Park, Lord and Lady Poltimore lived in the white-fronted slate-and-lead-roofed, originally Tudor mansion at the rear of the Park beyond the oak trees and the herds of deer. Some years later the house became a school for "superior young ladies" sometimes to be seen wandering in the grounds, and who, as the romantically minded but less superior young gentlemen from Pinhoe grew up, proved more of an attraction than the deer or the squirrels or even the conkers.

Later still, Poltimore House became a maternity home. Not that there was any connection between that change of use and those earlier flirtatious encounters on either side of the Park's high iron railings.

Since then the house's bad fortune has escalated, helped by a plague of interior dry rot followed by a questionable fire, though in this case the building survived, outwardly more or less intact. Some of the trees are still standing in the Park, though accommodating only grey squirrels instead of red. And the view from the tall elegant front windows of Poltimore House now encompasses that most offensive of rural desecrations: a motorway.

Some distance behind the house once lay an area of oak woodlands known as Old Park Woods. Many of its trees had been felled during the First World War, but leaving others sufficiently dense to shelter numbers of wild creatures, with shaded pathways through holly, rhododendron and bracken. But in the late 1930s, before the Second World War which might have provided some excuse for such an act of wholesale vandalism, the greater part of Old Park Woods was bulldozed and uprooted and carried away out of existence, leaving a vast acreage of farmland to replace those former acres of peaceful forest glades that breathed out life-sustaining oxygen and consuming CO_2, as well as providing cover for all manner of wild creatures and wild flowers.

Interestingly though, in accordance with today's more enlightened agricultural practices, an adjoining field has now been planted with trees. But it will be many hundreds of years before there is a new Old Park Wood.

Pinhoe School

ALL too soon, the time came for little Denny to start at his father's school, but after Mrs Stapleton, the Infants' Teacher, had seated him in a miniature chair at a miniature table beside a scarcely less miniature Stanley, his premonitory fears and terrors quickly faded. Stanley had been going to school for at least one term, and having learnt that he was to have "skulemaizder's zun" as a companion, had thoughtfully brought along a few pieces from his Meccano set to help make his new friend feel at home. There were also Freddy Causley and Raymond Jewell, all four of them roughly the same age.

There were seldom more than sixty or so pupils in the whole school, ranging in age from about five to fourteen, and divided into eight classes or "standards" shared between four teachers. The Infants practised their letters and numbers on slates: thin slabs about twelve inches by eight, lighter and thinner than the sort used on roofs, and contained in light wooden frames. The pencils were slender rods of the same material, about six inches long until they snapped, which they did pretty promptly when grasped in unskilled fists. At other times they made models from curiously perfumed Plasticine, or they cut shapes out of brightly coloured paper, using miniature scissors with safely rounded ends, and stuck them on to larger squares of grey sugar-paper which were hung around the classroom walls.

There were two classes of Infants grouped according to their ages, perhaps no more than twelve children altogether, and run separately from the rest of the school, with their own morning prayers and hymns led by Mrs Stapleton from a seat at a wheezy harmonium, and an entirely different playtime.

In between less academic activities came 'Rithmatic, when the second and older class chanted their "Times Tables" together, as far up as "Twelve":

> One Twelve is Twelve,
> Two Twelves is Twenny-four,
> Dree Twelves is Thurdy-zix,

and so on to the rather tricky

Twelve twelves is a 'undred-an'-vordy-vor!

Meanwhile, through the closed door leading to Standards One and Two, Miss Bessie Bagwell might be heard prompting both her Standards at their own somewhat adenoidal version of a choral Avourdupois:

Zixteen grains one dram,
Zixteen drams one ounce,
Zixteen ounces one pound,
Vordeen pounds one ztone . . .

and so on up to "one ton".

It required considerable mental concentration on the part of the classful of raggedly chanting reciters to avoid being distracted by the insistent counter-chanting coming from the other side of the heavy curtain that divided the main schoolroom into halves, when Miss Minnie Coles was putting her Standards Three and Four through today's no less archaic:

Vor gills one pint,
Two pints one quart,
Vor quarts one gallon,
Two gallons one peck,
Vor pecks one bushel,
Eight bushels one quarter . . .

And farther along again, on the other side of yet another closed door, this one leading to the headmaster's èlite thirteen and fourteen year olds in Standards Five and Six, twelve inches were one foot:

> Dree voot one yard,
> Vive-an'-a 'arf yards one rod, pole or perch,
> Zixty-zix voot one chain,
> Ten chains one vurlong,
> Eight vurlong

and here the rhythmic rise and fall of young voices would be broken into a more ragged

> — make one mile or
> One thousand seven 'undred and zixty yards, or
> Vive thousand two 'undred and eighty veet!

Also of course, two farthings made one ha'penny:

> Two 'a'pennies one penny,
> Twelve pennies one shilling,
> Twenny shillings one pound,
> Twenny-one shillings one guinea . . .

These tables, chorused in unison in song-song repetitive cadences, achieved a permanent mnemonic effect. Few children left Pinhoe School without knowing all about gills and pecks and chains and stones and bushels and their precise capacities, dimensions and usages, as well as the number of feet in a mile, and of elevens in one hundred-and-twenty-one.

There would be head-scratching, lip-biting written work in the form of a shopkeeper's account that first had to be painstakingly copied down from the blackboard:

Dr. to . . .			£ s. d.
¼ lb tea	@	1s.6d. per lb. . .	= . . . .
3lbs sugar	@	6d. per lb. . .	= . . . .
½ lb butter	@	10d. per lb. . .	= . . . .
¾ lb lard	@	4d. per lb. . .	= . . . .
1½ lbs bacon	@	7d. per lb. . .	= . . . .
1 stone potatoes	@	2d. per lb. . .	= . . . .

and so on, and the whole lot would have to be added up, remembering the foregoing tables. The prices may have been a bit arbitrary, perhaps because chalked up on the board by the teacher out of her head, but the processes of calculation and conversion were the same.

There were mental arithmetic problems like "How much is a ton of coal at 1s.6d. a hundredweight?" or "3 quarts milk at 2½d. a pint?" or "5 yards of ribbon at 4d. a foot?" Such mental acrobatics were required only of the older pupils. Mrs Stapleton's Infants were blissfully unaware of what was in store for them on the other side of that closed door.

Sometimes in the course of his 'Rithmatic lessons, Mr Jones would suddenly pick on someone suspected of inattentiveness or day dreaming and rudely wake them up with: "Seven times eight? Quick! . . ." "Inches in a yard?" . . . "Pecks in a bushel?" . . . and shame on them if they couldn't come up with the right answer straight away! Now and again he would try trick questions to keep everyone on their toes: "How many hundredweights in a quarter?" . . . "Furlongs in a chain?"

Multiplying, dividing, adding and subtracting all those bothersome £.s.d., those hotchpotches of bushels and pecks and quarters and pounds, those disparate assortments of lengths and distances: it was all sound brainworthy stuff, all part of the third of the obligatory basic "three Rs".

Despite the hard work of such brain teasers, perhaps the children really enjoyed them, taking a secret and perverse pride in being required to know them, all part of their inherent national superiority. There were no baby countable-on-fingers decimals in those days, though they were known to be in use in "vureign parts" like France, Germany and Spain. As was well understood by the patriotic five and six year old offspring of a race of wartime heroes, past and present, alive or dead, well grounded in Great Britain's history of habitually defeating the armed might of those other three countries, "them vureigners" could hardly be expected to cope with complicated methods of pricing and measurement and calculation like £.s.d. and inches and feet and yards, furlongs and chains, and eleven times eleven.

Not that the decimal system was completely ignored at Pinhoe School. With a certain amount of disdain,

9

Mr Jones's Standards Five and Six soon learnt to puzzle over the purposeless conversion of grams to ounces and pounds to kilograms. The ridiculous centimetre aroused a great deal of superior mirth, being only a fraction of an inch and having no other measures between it and the next size up, which was three and a third inches longer than a yard. In a way their minds were being prepared a good half century in advance for the diminution of their mental agility and that of their children, though they could never have suspected it.

Once or twice a year "Nurse" visited the school to inspect hands and heads, on the lookout for such endemic afflictions as warts, finger-nails bitten down to the quick, nits, lice and fleas. It was a thankless and unpleasant job, not only because of the odoriferous proximity of the unwashed juvenile bodies that it was her duty to inspect, but because she made her rounds of the local schools by bicycle and in whatever weather Nature chose to inconvenience her.

At Pinhoe School she usually got a good haul of unwanted live-stock from the heads of the "poorer classes": those children who lived in unideal conditions at Blackall or "Slum" Court, or under the flea-infested thatch of the fire-doomed cob cottages beside the main road. What the unwitting harbourers of those creatures made of the little bottles of lotions and disinfectant Nurse left with them for use at home there was no knowing. Only once did an irate mother turn up the morning after to return the unused bottle, claiming its contents were not fit to drink.

Poor Bessie Bagwell, as the most junior of the teachers, often found herself performing the functions of subsidiary nurse during the intervals between the real nurse's visits, combing through the hair of a suspect host, usually one of the girls whose long tangled tresses provided ideal hatcheries. She would seat her on a chair just inside the porch and utter exclamations of fastidious disapproval every time she picked something out from the teeth of the comb to squash between scraps of newspaper, these operations being followed with surreptitious interest by the rest of her two classes who of course were supposed to be "getting on" with the work she had set them.

A doctor and a dentist also paid occasional visits to the school, which caused great anticipatory anxiety among the children. For the doctor's attentions most of them turned up in their best clothes, or at any rate unstitched themselves, or were unstitched by their mothers, from their undergarments: full-length "coms" which, provided with appropriate slits and holes, were kept on day and night, week in week out, throughout the whole period of the cold winter months.

There were cloakrooms opening up from the rear of every classroom, heavy with geoponic odours from the outdoor coats and hats hanging up there on wet days. The outside lavatories, lined with heavy slabs of slate under a corrugated iron roof, stood at the far side of two narrow yards, one for the Infants and girls, the other for the boys and separated from each other by a high wall which it was the lingering ambition of some of the older boys to climb over.

Most of the older children had a rough idea of the facts of life, gathered from older brothers and sisters or the habits of pet rabbits, cats, dogs and farm animals. Very occasionally one or two of them dared to try them out for themselves — a brother and a sister in the privacy of their own communal bedroom, or in barns, garden sheds or behind haystacks.

Out in the school playground while the boys were engaged in their rumbustious games of "vootball" and the younger ones were Red Indians or bandits or escaping prisoners of the recent war, the girls played hopscotch roughly chalked out as far away from the vootball as possible, and various games with skipping ropes, all usually accompanied by cheerful little jingles:

> Mother, may I go down to swim?
> Ees, my darling dor-ter.
> 'Ang your clo'es on yon-der tree
> But don't go near the wa-ter!'

or:
> My mother said
> I never should
> play with the gyp-sies
> In the wood.
> If I did
> She would say
> Naught-y girl
> To dis-o-*bey!*

One of Mrs Stapleton's many pleasing practices was the award of a farthing to each of her diminutive charges in turn: for good work, good behaviour, "trying hard", fetching teacher's (or 't'cher's) umbrella from the cloakroom if it was raining, or failing any of that, simply because a child's turn for it had come round. The farthing, eagerly grasped in a clammy fist, was soon transmuted into something else at Mrs Bindon's, not much of which would be left by the time its purchaser got back. What remained might be shared round the class. A farthing, known in the vernacular as a "varden", was good for at least an ounce of suitably small and thus numerous "comfits" or "dolly mixtures".

Mrs Bindon's shop was strategically positioned immediately opposite the school entrance. To the children it was an Aladdin's Cave, its two bow windows given over exclusively to sweets and toys, the latter ranging from whipping-tops and skipping-ropes, cartons of highly coloured clay marbles, tin cap-pistols and little cast-iron bombs and rolls of mildly explosive caps to go with them, each no bigger than a parsnip seed, to novelties of various kinds: flip-over "movies", comic masks, and sheets of transfers that produced instant tattooings on hands and bare arms and knees.

The highly pungent interior of Mrs Bindon's was entered via a door with a loudly pinging bell, and was crammed with items of more interest to grown-ups. A three-foot high tower consisting of slabs of grey salt fish stood just inside the doorway, with nearly always a black cat curled up asleep on the topmost slab. Ladies' "unmentionables" were displayed none too discreetly at one end of the counter while a pair of brass scales with its attendant brass weights stood at the other. On the floor were sacks of onions and potatoes, dried peas and beans, loose tea, rice, sugar and flour. There were household utensils and garden tools, earthenware "charlies" in their straw wrappings, and a drum of paraffin in one corner with its measuring-jug and filling-funnel beside it.

Mrs Bindon was as apple-cheeked and good-natured as Mrs Stapleton, if perhaps rather more dumpy. They might almost have been sisters; they looked alike and were similarly kindly. From behind her counter Mrs Bindon would greet her juvenile customers and their familiar "vardens'-worth" requirements with a motherly smile, then reach into the back of her window for the indicated wide-stoppered glass jar and tip it over the pear-shaped brass bowl of her scales, which she always allowed to drop down well past the level. She would take a square of brown paper from beneath the counter, twist it deftly into a cone, pour comfits or 'undreds-an'-thousands or jelly babies or dolly mixtures into it, tuck in the "pig's ear" at the top of the cone and hand it over. "There y'are, me dear. Mind 'ow you crosses the road, now!"

Not that there was very much traffic about then: perhaps a lumbering solid-tyred wooden-seated Devon General omnibus plying between Exeter and Cullumpton, a traction-engine showering sparks from its tall funnel and iron-ribbed wheels, a young fellow on his cow-horn-handlebarred Douglas with his cap on backwards, or a dashing young farmer in a smart pony-drawn gig.

14

But the school children were subject to punishments as well as rewards, though only in "Infants" was the reward the gift of a varden. Every teacher kept a cane in her desk — a short length of garden bamboo — except Mrs Stapleton, who used a short nine-inch ruler tapped sharply but lightly on a reluctantly extended palm. The shame and disgrace brought tears to Infant eyes, rather than real pain. Only in extreme cases, like "Nasty's" excesses, was an offender sent to Headmaster Jones and made to "bend over".

The latter punishment only applied to boys, in any case. Girls seldom made serious nuisances of themselves; their offences were usually matters of spite or cattiness. A girl was generally the choice for monitor, a temporary honour bestowed when a teacher needed to leave her class during a lesson. The monitor stood in front of the class like a teacher, her duties being to keep order and report any misdemeanours to the teacher on her return. This lent itself to a certain amount of childish vindictiveness when an outraged accused "offender" (usually, but not always, a boy) would protest in his defence "Ooh, Miss, I never!"

Canings, on the palm of the hand or lower down, were accepted with philosophical resignation by others besides the recipients themselves. Children deserved their punishments, in view of what they so often got away with. No parent would have dreamt of complaining (to whom: Mr Jones himself, the vicar-chairman of managers, or the education authority at Exeter?) about the supposed indignities inflicted on their offspring (assuming they ever heard about them), any more than Henry VIII's subjects would have dared to complain about his treatment of them. School teachers were regarded as "edicated"; at least, above the average for the village; and therefore knew best how to deal with children. And the children themselves seemed to thrive on the treatment. Of those most frequently required to "bend over", most did pretty well in later life, though some first moved on to secondary schools where they ran the routine gauntlet of "the whack" instead. But all of them profitted from their grounding in "reading" and "'riting" and "£.s.d", and "avoirdupois" until the latter complex systems were abandoned in favour of Europe's elementary decimals. Fred Gee and Nasty were two who did not turn out well, despite their constant thrashings. But even Mr Jones had to have his failures.

Mrs Bindon's husband, her second, was the village coalman, with two horses, two flat sideless coal-carts and George Hallet from Playmoor Cottage to drive the second one. George Hallet was a dour individual in the habit of flicking his whip at boys who tried to steal lifts on the back of his empty cart; an unfriendly gesture which his employer, Mrs Bindon's easy-going husband, perhaps because more tolerant of her regular varden or even 'a'penny customers, was never guilty of. His depot was at the goods siding on the other side of the level-crossing from the railway station. There is still a coal depot there today, but not Mr Bindon's, and no longer supplied from open wagons of coal that had been loaded at coal-pit sidings in Mr Jones's South Wales.

Mr Bindon had a son, Henry, by his first wife, an ex-Royal Navy stoker, survivor of three separate torpedoings, who was intent on profiting from those three lucky escapes by turning himself into a safely land-bound motor-mechanic and garage owner. Henry had a corner at one end of his father's coal office next to his stepmother's shop, where he mended bicycles — usually their punctures — and from a hand-operated pump outside, near his father's weighbridge, dispensed Pratts' "ethyl" to those of the local élite who possessed motors.

Henry worked all hours, and scrimped and saved for years to buy a motor of his own. Yet somehow he still found time to play in Pinhoe's Association Football Club's cup-winning team. He got on very well with Mrs Bindon who, unlike the traditional stepmother of nursery tales, could not have looked after him better if he had been her own son.

Perhaps because of that Henry never bothered to get married. When eventually he retired he went to live with his then-widowed stepmother in the bungalow he had built for her a little way down Pinn Court Farm Lane. But long before then he had worked up a highly successful petrol filling station and repair garage, had bought his father a motor lorry to replace the horses and carts and had even taught George Hallet to drive it (without his whip), and an enormous American Dodge for himself for hire and taxi work.

CHAPTER TWO

The Parish Vicar, Chairman of School Managers
While the village headmaster exercised an influence
and enjoyed a degree of respect seldom accorded his
successors three quarters of a century later, by far the
most colourful character in the village was its vicar.

After first studying and then abandoning Medicine,
Mr Oliver Puckridge opted for the Church. Having
become a "Reverend", in 1902 he took up the
incumbency at Pinhoe. By the 1920s, the length of
time he had been there gave him an edge on almost
everyone else in the parish. He had officiated at the
christenings, confirmation preparations, weddings and
funerals of so many of his flock, it was perhaps not
surprising that he seemed to regard his position as
Christ's personal representative and earthly go-
between more literally than might be approved by his
Bishop. His closed three-fingered benediction (closed
fingers in token of the three-in-one-Trinity) was
bestowed on his regular church-attending parishioners,
while backsliders and chapel-goers, being beyond the
pale, were consigned to the Devil by its omission. As
for his own frail flesh, it gave every indication of being
immortal. His daily diet was spartanly healthful:
oatmeal gruel without milk or sugar, brown butterless
bread, dried apple-rings, a date or a fig (products of the

Holy Land) and a weekly top-up of the Chalice towards the close of Holy Communion to warm the cockles of his hale old heart.

Not only were there very few in the village who could recall when he was not its vicar and consequently Chairman of the School's Board of Managers, but few except the very youngest were likely to live long enough to see the day when he would cease to be either. The sequel to his apparently unlikely demise, which was "to sit at the right hand of the Lord God in His Kingdom in Heaven" was, however, more than once confidently prognosticated by him to his congregation.

To say that the Reverend O. Puckridge was eccentric would be to understate the facts. The less said about some of his oddities, the better. His faithful wife and helper, Fanny, had had to put up with them for years, perhaps since their marriage in 1893, so why not the whole parish? Not the least of their joint sorrows had been the loss of their son Christopher, killed in "the War" — that great non-respecter of persons and the feelings of their loved ones. His name is on the granite Memorial in his father's churchyard and on a brass tablet in the wall inside the church beside the pulpit.

By the 1920s poor Fanny was stone deaf, a circumstance that sometimes gave people the impression in public that her husband was haranguing her vehemently. In church on Sundays she sat in a front pew immediately beneath the pulpit and lip-read adoringly every word of the sermons (most of them extempore and tending to dwell on the least delicate aspects of Biblical transgression), which her husband

19

enlarged on in his quavering liturgical tones to a bemused congregation.

Old Oliver had two modes of transport besides his own black-gaitered and black-booted shanks. One was his bicycle, a unique machine provided with a "back-pedalling brake", an internal expanding device at that time not yet being fitted to every motor vehicle, a four-speed gear with a foot-long operating lever more suitable for a motor-cycle, and a large flat triangular leather case that exactly fitted inside the triangle of the frame. In this case he kept a set of ecclesiastical vestments for emergency use on his pastoral visits, a current copy of the *Church Times* and a paper bag of dried apple-rings to sustain him on his journeys. He also had a kind of map-holder clamped to the handlebars, but which instead of a map held a Bible, prayer-book or other devotional volume, its pages kept open by means of an elastic band.

On this machine old Oliver demonstrated his faith in the Lord's reluctance to summon him to a seat beside Him straight away. In blazer and mortar-board, his usual fine-weather garb, he would come hurtling down the one-in-seven decline of Church Hill, eyes on the fluttering sacred pages in front of him, the tassel on his mortar-board streaming behind him like a Chinaman's pigtail in a typhoon. He would swing blindly round The Corner into the main road, or else go straight across it into Station Road or Langaton Lane. He never looked where he was going and over more than forty years he never had an accident, so there may be something to say for his faith in his Lord's forbearance, or else in the evasive skills of other road users.

On occasions he cycled to Exeter, forgot that he had done so and caught the train back to Pinhoe, having left his bike propped against the pavement in a city street. There it would remain overnight or sometimes for days on end, until someone from the village, perhaps a local farmer driving past in his gig or a tradesman in his van, would recognise it, bring it back and restore it to its owner. That sort of thing could not happen today.

The vicar's other mode of transport was his donkey Michael, named after the church's patron saint. Michael usually found himself between the shafts of a small two-wheeled cart, a cross between the sort of soap-box go-cart young boys liked to trundle themselves about in and a scaled-down version of an Ancient British chariot. Like both of those, it was provided with no springs.

Every Friday morning during term-time the vicar arrived at the village school in this donkey-cart to "take Holy Scripture", not to "take it" in the sense of teach it, but to satisfy himself that the subject was being properly taken by the teachers. Pinhoe Elementary School being a Church of England establishment, the vicar was automatically Chairman of its four-man Board of Managers and so in a sense one of Headmaster Jones's employers — the others being found in the offices of the Local Education Authority at the Castle in Exeter. As representative of the Church, it was one of the vicar's responsibilities to oversee what was optimistically termed "the spiritual welfare" of the children.

The children themselves, supremely indifferent to their spiritual welfare, would soon have made havoc of Mr Puckridge's visits if each teacher had not remained in the classroom with him to keep order. The headmaster had privately little sympathy for the vicar, being frequently at odds with him, always on the losing side, over matters of school routine, the upkeep of the school building, and non-scholastic events that were held in that building during evenings and holidays, Saturday-night dances continuing past midnight into the Sabbath, for instance. But despite being an influential member of the National Union of Teachers he still had the Chairman of Managers' assessment of him to bear in mind, and no pupil dared to misbehave in front of the Reverend Oliver Puckridge when Mr Jones was in the background.

One year, on the Friday before Palm Sunday, the vicar arrived at the school astride his donkey without its cart, arrayed in his ecclesiastical vestments, feet all but touching the ground (Oliver being lean and tall, and Michael no bigger than a Shetland pony). Whether as one of Christ's accredited representatives on earth he expected to be greeted with hosannas and sprays of ash-tree leaves (the nearest thing to palm fronds in the Pinhoe area) was not altogether clear. Perhaps he was only trying to give the children a first-hand illustration of that 2,000-year-old event but it did not go down very well with the headmaster and his three assistants, who considered it to be in poor taste if not actually sacriligious.

In between wandering through the school from classroom to classroom to check on the children's

22

familiarity with prayer-book and Bible, he liked to tell them about a memorable episode in the early history of Pinhoe, which explained his ownership of the donkey that had conveyed him to school that morning and which at the moment would be tied up to the chestnut palings at one side of the playground, contentedly grazing on empty paper bags and discarded apple cores.

The story went back only about half as far as that of Christ's entry into Jerusalem — to AD 1001. Throughout the four or five centuries after the breakdown of the Roman Empire and particularly at the time of Ethelred the Unready's disastrous reign, the Vikings had been busily engaged in treating the usurping Saxons to frequent tastes of their own medicine.

What became known as the Battle of Pinhoe followed an abortive attack on Exeter, which was still able to shelter behind the remains of its Roman walls. It took place somewhere north of the present church on or around the eminence now known as Beacon Down. The local *fyrds* had begun to run short of arrows and the parish priest hurried to Exeter on his donkey for fresh supplies, returning in time for the Saxons to bring about one of their rare victories over the invaders.

For this service he was awarded a yearly stipend of one mark in perpetuity (about 13s.4d. or 66p) by the grateful Bishop and burghers of the city, properly speaking for the upkeep of the donkey, regarded as the real hero of the day. How subsequent incumbents of the parish down the centuries used the award the vicar

23

did not say. But it appealed to his sense of fairness that since he continued to receive it, it should be put to its proper purpose. Hence, Michael.

Having thus learnt about the Battle of Pinhoe, and further inspired by reading about the Vikings and seeing pictures of their armour in the school's history primers, Denny and his constant companion Stanley set off one fine Saturday morning to search for souvenirs among the remains of the Danish victims of that 900-year-old event.

They went with high hopes and a sack and spade and pickaxe. The site was well enough known, having been "dug", without result, by the local historical association (of which Mr Jones was predictably a member) some years earlier in 1923. Its locality was, and still is, known as Danes' Wood, otherwise Mincimore Copse, no more than a quarter mile below the minor cross-roads at Cheyney Gate. But despite their hopes of bronze helmets and shields and swords and battle-axes, the boys unearthed only a few rusty tins and a broken milk bottle, though the suspected tumulus and the trenches cut across it, in the manner of the 1920s, were still visible among the tangled root systems of numerous trees.

Probably they and the experts before them had been looking in the wrong place. There is another Danes' Wood marked on the OS map a few miles farther east, not far from Killerton, no great distance from the supposed scene of battle, skirmish and victorious pursuit. There is no record that any dig has been conducted there. Casual excavation of its several sandy humps reveal plenty of what geologists might call "iron pan", but nothing in the way of eleventh-century bronze and iron weaponry. But perhaps after all it has been dug before, unofficially; hence the little untidy sand-pits there.

Church Choir and Wolf Cubs

Two laudable organisations provided regular if disparate weekly diversions for the youth of the village and school, though neither did much to keep them out of mischief. In fact, the regular attendance required by both resulted in more irregular behaviour than is likely to have been anticipated by the devoted traditionalists in charge of the one or the idealistic innovator of the other.

The church choir and the village Wolf Cub Pack were made up largely of the same boys, although a basic requirement for the former was to possess, if not great musical talent, a least a reasonably tonal ear and a voice to go with it. The initial tests for this were carried out at school by Mr Jones, himself blessed with a modest tenor inherited from his Celtic past.

Regular singing lessons were part of the school curriculum, and at times when teenage trebles in Mr Puckridge's choir began to waver and fail Headmaster Jones would pick on likely replacements during singing lessons, his ear disconcertingly close to each open mouth in turn, while Miss Bessie Bagwell soft-pedalled an accompaniment in the background.

Quite a few were always passed over as out of the question. But one or two in due course would join

Pinhoe Church Choir, when the vicar and his organist-choirmaster John Laskey would make what they could of the latest oral and moral headaches that Headmaster Jones had inflicted on them.

Choir practices, held weekly on Thursdays evenings, took place not at the Parish Church a good mile from the village up the steep hill named after it, but at a building known as the Mission Church, occasionally used for early morning Communion services, in the centre of the village. This Mission Church still stands besides the main road, wall-deep in a clutter of late twentieth century eyesores, a thick-buttressed building, formerly cream-washed but now grey, which back in the mid-1800s housed the village school. In the mid-1900s it still housed, along with its rows of dark wooden pews and its wooden altar, an ancient harmonium, cousin perhaps to the one in Mrs Stapleton's classroom. Every Thursday evening John Laskey pedalled out from Exeter on his bicycle, to pedal and squeeze on this harmonium his practice selections for the forthcoming Sunday's services of praise and supplication, while frequently supplicating but seldom praising the junior members of his choir.

The junior members habitually did their best to get into the Mission Church before anyone else, in order to rummage in a cupboard behind the vestry curtain and help themselves to swigs from a bottle of Communion Sacramento, which no doubt added gusto and flavour to their subsequent signing, if little improvement to tonality or timbre.

Of that singing — their rendering of hymns and psalms, canticles, responses and amens — there is no record, which is perhaps just as well. The boys were not of the calibre and capability of the groups of immature angels who graced the chancel stalls of such a temple of spiritual euphony as Exeter Cathedral. The boys of St Michael's Church Choir, Pinhoe, in Denny's days, if not before and after, were no better than a gang of deplorable ragamuffins in unconvincing disguise. They wore Eton collars and clip-on bow-ties, long black cassocks and short, briefly snow-white surplices, under which were stuffed into mucky trouser pockets cigarette fag-ends, purely — or impurely — status-enhancing French letters, marbles, and grasshoppers in match-boxes (the two latter to be set bouncing and leaping over the tiles of the chancel floor during old Oliver's lengthy sermons) and other even less hygienic possessions. Even the adult congregation would grow restive during sermons, so it was not surprising that the choirboys did.

As the church was a long up-hill mile or so from the village, a long and noisy up-hill mile or so it was for those phony exponents of tattered hymnals and grubby-thumbed Psalters. Catapulting and stone-kicking and quarrelling their way up between the high weedy hedges past the entrance to Hammett's malodorous piggeries (now Sheila O'Brien's Riding Centre, teetering on the northern brink of Tarmac Brick's enormous clay-pit) and loitering in gateways for unmentionable purposes amid wafts of illicit Woodbine fumes, they would be passed by members of the congregation, straggling by with averted disapproving eyes.

They primed their mucky minds and imperilled their immature souls, if they had any, with gems of rustic scatological humour, in ill-considered contrast to the declarations of adulation and supplication they were shortly to be chanting in the name of a surely undeceived Maker.

"Wot's the 'ight of impossibility?" was a well-worked riddle (something to do with a postage stamp and part of an elephant's anatomy). — "Why do male monkeys like living in Africa?" (even worse).

Or intriguing book-titles by appropriate authors: "*King Solomon's Wives* by Ridem Haggard." — "*A Race for the Throne* by Mustapha Krapp."

Sunday after Sunday one of their number, Dick by name, repeatedly started to tell a long, involved and presumably dirty story, but was never able to get beyond the first few sentences before doubling up with helpless laughter at the funniness of it, which thus was never conveyed to anyone else. The rest of the boys tried to take it in good part, indulgently laughing at the fact that he was laughing, though it was frustrating never to hear the end of Dick's dirty story. But in any case, it helped to fill the time on the way up Church Hill *en route* for the vestry and their waiting vestments.

Warned by the change from Plain Bobs to the slow tolling of the five-minute bell from the louvres of the ancient sandstone tower, some public-spirited individual among the boys — Lionel, Les, George, Stan, 'Arry, or Dick (if he had stopped laughing by then) —

would hand round a tiny tin of black mentholated "Imps" with which to defumigate breaths that were shortly to be profaning the sacred air between altar and rood-screen.

Sometimes they miscalculated the time they had taken coming up from the village and arrived at the church too early, when they would don the underpart of their ritual disguise, their long black cassocks, and then slip outside again to the older part of the graveyard and start noisy games of "touch" and "tag" among the moss-grown stones and table-tombs, looking and sounding not unlike a more infernal sort of imp, mocking the ancient dead and the devout living. The latter by then would be in their pews and at their preliminary prayers, and one of the sidesmen would get up and tiptoe out to the vestry to complain about the hooting and screaming going on outside. Then an irate John Laskey, backed up by a couple of strong-armed tenors or basses, would go out to the graveyard and grab a few cassock collars and box a few ears and so put a stop to the unholy junketings.

An effort was made to get poor stone-deaf Fanny Puckridge to occupy these early arrivals with a kind of Bible Class, doomed from the moment of its inception by the cruel advantage the little savages took of her sad disability.

Meanwhile, Len Butt, Pinhoe's tiler and thatcher, possessor of a gammy leg acquired at his hazardous occupation, who gamely limped up Church Hill twice daily, fine weather or foul, would take up his post where the back of the organ did not quite reach the end of the north wall of the chancel. Part-time sexton, grave-digger and organ-blower, he would settle a pair of steel-rimmed spectacles on his nose and prepare himself with prayer-book, hymn book and Psalter propped up in front of him to keep pace with the liturgical needs of John Laskey, on the keyboard side of the organ. A wooden bar projecting from a vertical slot at the back of the instrument needed to be pumped up and down a few times whenever a small plumb-bob on the end of a thin wire on a pulley showed the pressure in the bellows inside to be dropping.

The end part of the carved rood-screen on his right had been boarded up, perhaps to conceal him from the congregation or *vice versa*; but Len Butt had scooped out a little peep-hole in the woodwork to give him a one-way view of the congregation and, to keep him further alerted to the organist's requirements, to watch the movements of the worshippers in the act of standing up or kneeling down or resuming their seats.

Now and again the services of the choirboys were required for a funeral. This was a rate treat for the little horrors, who were paid extra for the privilege, which in any case meant an afternoon off from school.

Rigged out in their Sunday best and agog with unsuppressible excitement, they made a special point of arriving early — not so much in hope of a preliminary game of tag or of fortifying their pagan hearts against the presence of Death with sly swigs of Sacramento, but to give them plenty of time to admire the bier waiting empty at the lynch-gate and then to troop off and inspect the open grave. This would be tastefully lined with laurel and rhododendron leaves, a painstaking embellishment for which Len Butt no doubt hoped to be rewarded by one of the mourners.

One of the older choirboys, Albert, was evidently curious as to what his own internment might look like, if not feel, like in a hopefully far-distant future, for on one occasion he jumped the six feet down to the bottom of a waiting grave and looked up, grinning.

"Cor — it's orright down 'ere!" a claim which seemed exaggerated, to say the very least. The rest of them, though by no means a queasy lot, seemed happy to take him at his word and not try it for themselves.

The choirboys were paid sixpence for every Sunday's full attendance: threepence a service, twenty-six shillings a year. But although John Laskey sat at his keyboard with his back to the choir, he was able to keep a watchful eye on them by means of a tell-tale mirror fixed over his battery of stops, and would enter in a little notebook the names of those he saw misbehaving, each earning a threepenny fine, so that all too often many of the choirboys would find themselves doing their Sunday stint for nothing.

The Wolf Cub Pack was, of course, not much better behaved, seeing that it consisted of the very same boys, augmented by those whose tone-deaf groans and croaks had disqualified them from the choir. The route to "Cubs" lay up the same Church Hill, a further quarter-mile past the side-turning to the church, to the stable-block belonging to Beacon Down House, the home of Lady Hull. Akela, the Cub Mistress, was Lady

Hull's daughter Barbara. The clubhouse or "lair" was a disused tack-room at one end of the stables. To get to this lair meant running the gauntlet of the rear ends of two or three high-spirited hunters, and sometimes the ire of their groom, who clearly did not like boys, or at any rate did not like this lot, Wolf Cubs or not.

"Git away from them 'arses!" he would greet them cantankerously if he happened to be about when they turned up. (Little could he have suspected that half a dozen years later as huntsman at Silverton Kennels, not a mile away, he would be giving unofficial riding lessons to one of those former Wolf Cubs at half a crown a time.)

While the Cubs waited in the disused tack-room for Miss Barbara to arrive there was all manner of interesting rubbish and household junk to rummage about in. Not much of it had anything to do with tack or with Scouting or Wolf Cubs: there was a rusty breech mechanism from an ancient rifle complete with hammer and percussion-nipple, an old carriage lantern dating no doubt from the days before Miss Barbara's motor car, besides sundry bits of broken harness and saddlery. There were moth-eaten hunting and shooting trophies: glass-eyed foxes's masks, a stag's head lacking one of its antlers, the remains of a stuffed eagle in a smashed glass case.

There was a tiny fireplace at one end of the tack-room by which the grooms and stable lads of former days would have sat on early winter mornings while cleaning and soaping and polishing leather and brass and steel in preparation for a coming meet. The Wolf

Cubs practised their fire-lighting skills in the fireplace, stuffing it with old newspaper and bits of rotten wood. After vain but vociferous attempts to light it by the time-honoured if mythical method of rubbing two sticks together and then failing no less decisively with a stone struck against the blade of a Boy Scout clasp-knife, they would resort to one of their precious choirboy-fag-lighting Swan Vestas, and crouch around feeding the flames with yet more mouldy paper and rotten wood.

Akela never seemed to mind that when she arrived she would find her cublings had been making free with whatever they had unearthed in that frowsty lair. She would come in, neat in regulation khaki skirt and blouse and fluttering ribbons and insignia, bringing with her the pack's totem-pole, a wolf's head of fretwork mounted on a broomstick, to be greeted by her two clamorous packs prancing about in green and yellow caps and jerseys and scarves, all eager to squat and bob and DYB and DOB and salute with two fingers splayed out like wolf cubs' ears above their own right ears. She was one of those well-meaning members of the minor aristocracy who considered it part of their duty to DO THEIR OWN BEST for those placed lower down the social and financial ladder than themselves.

There was a small wood in the grounds of Beacon Down House where with much hooting and whistling and unconvincing bird and animal calls, the Cubs would practise their stalking and woodcraft, and where at Easter Akela would hide an appropriate number of chocolate eggs in the naive hope, seldom realised, that each of her Cubs would conveniently find one each.

On one memorable occasion she piled both packs of six into her open Wolseley tourer, the overflow standing on the running-board and clinging to the sides, and drove the two miles into Exeter to see *The Retreat from Mons* at the Plaza cinema. This was a silent film, made up from a combination of genuine hand-cranked 1914 news film and some acted episodes. It was of particularly poignant interest to Miss Barbara and the rest of her family, since it was at during the Retreat that her father, a Lieutenant-General, had been killed.

Once or twice the Cubs were admitted into the House, tiptoeing respectfully through the great entrance hall hung about with big-game heads and native weaponry and other evidence of the late Earl's pre-war interests, to Akela's old playroom. The purpose of the visit would be to watch a magic-lantern show depicting various aspects of Scouting Life. A parlour maid in black and frilly white cap and apron would appear halfway through the performance with a tray of biscuits and lemonade for the audience, and Lady Hull herself look in benevolently from the doorway.

Once — and once was enough — the Wolf Cubs attended a week-long Jamboree camp at Thorverton, travelling there in style in the back of Henry Bindon's first motor lorry. A miserable wet and windy affair it was, too; typical August weather in no way relieved by the presence of numerous eminent High Ups: Chiefs and Deputy Chiefs, Presidents, Commissioners and so on, amongst whom the younger daughter of Lady Hull was very small fry indeed, let alone her two packs of cubs.

The cooking was done on open fires in the open air, despite the rain, authentic Boy Scout style, with porridge in huge dixies like cauldrons borrowed from the local witch or brought back from cannibal country by explorers like Colonel Fawcett (of Stoke Canon and the Amazon jungle), invariably burnt (again, despite the rain) and bread and fried eggs predictably soggy and leathery.

Wolf Cubs and Boy Scouts and Scouters and Rovers and Scout-Masters (there must have been hundreds of them from all over the county) slept in ex-Army bell tents that lacked their essential wooden floorboards. Rain fell incessantly, most of it coming straight through the rotten canvas, soaking ground-sheets and blankets and their shivering occupants.

Scoutmasters and Rovers set splendid examples to the youngsters, splashing about under flapping inadequate capes, DOING THEIR BEST in accordance with Scout Law to "smile and whistle under all difficulties"; a requirement involving facial and labial contortions impossible to achieve at one and the same time, as two or three disloyal "tenderfeet" from the Pinhoe packs daringly demonstrated to each other as they slipped and slithered about on the wet grass and muddy paths, hoping to have constipated themselves on the burnt porridge and leathery eggs in order to avoid the nightmare latrines.

These latter, discreetly hidden behind brown canvas screens, were sinister open trenches railed off from their brinks by horizontal poles supported on short forked uprights. But Wolf Cubs and Scouts and Scout-Masters came in different sizes with different lengths of leg, leaving smaller Cubs to sit perched precariously on the poles, trousers round their ankles, feet well off the ground. This was bad enough in broad daylight when it was not raining; but at night in the dark in pouring rain and the edges of the trenches slippery with mud . . .

Predictably, Wilfred, the smallest member of the Pinhoe pack, taken short in the middle of a particularly wild wet night after over-indulgence in hoped-for antidotes to Boy Scout cookery, which had been purchased earlier on at the camp's tuck tent, had to fall in.

Back at Beacon Down one evening the Cubs came upon a complex arrangement of tanks and pipes like a miniature gas-works behind the stables. And that, as Akela told them, was exactly what it was: an acetylene lighting plant for the house. The Cubs already knew about the stuff called carbide and the inflammable gas that resulted when water was added to it. Most car lamps were still in the carbide-and-water era, while acetylene lamps for push bikes were highly desirable but well beyond their modest means.

Mains gas would never be brought up the three or four hundred feet to Beacon Down House, and mains electricity those days was out of the question. But in common with her contemporaries in the district,

36

Lady Hull eventually installed a motor-driven generator, and the gas-works behind the stables fell into disuse.

The house itself was an imposing mansion of white Portland stone commanding views over the lower Clyst and Exe rivers and their estuary, with the heights of Woodbury and Haldon on each side. It offered a far more prominent landmark for ships coming up the estuary than the church tower, which was a hundred feet below it but, unlike the house, marked on navigation charts. For this prominence, its occupants paid a heavy penalty.

The house was taken over by the RAF in 1940, and in April 1942 it was "taken out" by a unit of Lüftflotte 3, with disconcerting accuracy, considering the claim that its bombs were jettisoned in haste to avoid the vengeful attentions of a Polish night-fighter, rather than dropped because of the military importance of the target. Its modern replacement is sadly unworthy of its predecessor. One wonders how planning permission was granted for the glittering, glazed, brash-fronted monstrosity that stands there now. Viewed distantly from the south it resembles the front of a factory, and a badly designed factory at that. A landmark still, no question of that, but one that leaves an ugly mark on the land.

A sort of miniature palace now standing in the field below, where fifty years back "Gypsy" Penfold built his own bungalow and he and his daughter Christiana grazed their stallions and mares, would have made a more appropriate replacement for Beacon Down House if only it had been built on that loftier site.

Lady Hull suffered the loss of her family home, and her daughter-in-law was badly injured in the blitz of May 4th. But both must have been proud of Field Marshal Sir Richard Hull, Queen's Equerry and Lord Lieutenant of Devon, only son of the one and husband of the other, just as all three of them must have been proud of his soldier father. In her will Lady Hull left a bequest for the refurbishment of the organ in St Michael's Church, a more fitting memorial to the Hull family than the contemporary eyesore that blights the spot where once she stood in her warm spacious hall, while her daughter's Wolf Cubs tiptoed respectfully past to watch a magic lantern show about Scouting Life.

Lady Hull on her hill, comparatively remote from the village if not from the attentions of her country's enemies was, as a member of the aristocracy, the leading representative of the local gentry. A number of comfortably-off widows and maiden ladies of impeccable background lived on and around the outskirts of Pinhoe, from Broadparks to Pilton, Harrington, Wootton, Monkerton, Blackhorse, and Langaton. Many of the unmarried women were sisters. There were the Misses Pidsley, the Misses Melhuish, the Misses Coles, the Misses Chorley, the Misses Harrison and the Misses Livesey. Most were sad relics of romances shattered by the recent War, but whose private circumstances left them (unlike Miss Dash) with no need to make do with a second best.

All these were fairly regular attenders at Oliver Puckridge's church and thus assured of his regular three-fingered benediction. The three Coles sisters from Wootton sang in the ladies' section of the choir. One sad young lady still not in her thirties, a Miss Ridd (echo of the hero of *Lorna Doone*), was often to be seen on foot in Station Road on the way to or from the Post Office or the dairy, and on Sundays no less often at both morning and evening services.

Miss Dorothy Bedell fell into a different category, though it was not unlikely that she too had entertained earlier hopes of marriage. Dorothy's father, another of the managers of the school, was a well-to-do retired farmer from Pinn Court with a house, Parker's Cross, newly built beside the main road. His daughter was only ever seen on her horse. Not that the two were inseparable. The horse was often to be seen without her, grazing on one of her father's fields, looking so appallingly sway-backed as to give ample proof that its owner and rider was to state it mildly, over-weight. Quite a lot of women who rode seem to suffer from that complaint, so that one always felt sorry for the poor animals that had to carry them. Dorothy Bedell was never known to go to church, perhaps because there would have been nowhere to tether her means of getting there.

The gentlemen of the parish were as much in preponderance as the ladies, though for the most part were not such dedicated church-goers. Foremost among the genuine gentlemen of the district was dear old Arthur Dew, who lived in the tumbledown, formerly monastic Monkerton Manor at the lower end of the village, hard by the tiny Pinn Brook and just past its little stone bridge.

Arthur Dew was yet another member of the Management Board of the school, though like the rest, for no more than four years at a time under its permanent Chairman, Oliver Puckridge. But he was unquestionably the most colourful and benevolent of them.

Monkerton Manor, which Denny visited on more than one occasion in company with his father, the latter on school business, was a veritable Golconda packed with treasures and curios acquired by its owner during sojourns in China, Japan and India. One entered the house by an ancient mediœval doorway and was immediately transported into a kind of private museum. There were spears and shields, swords, muskets, knives, animals' heads, tables inlaid with ivory and mother-of-pearl, tapestries, punkahs, and every sort of heathen idol in every sort of material, including gold. One could hardy move about, let alone sit down in rooms so cluttered with priceless souvenirs.

Arthur Dew delighted in talking about them, doing his best to enlighten the small boy as well as the father on their usually gruesome history and origins. Once, when Mrs Jones accompanied her husband and young son to take tea with him and his invalid wife, he presented her with a huge diamond and ruby ring, after some trouble picking out one small enough to fit her finger. It had belonged to an Indian Rajah, so he informed her. It must have been worth a fortune, she had protested, and perhaps it was.

Headmaster Jones made much of a story told him by Arthur Dew, who had retired from the Royal Navy with the rank of Captain. When a sub-lieutenant he had been in charge of a gun team sent to relieve the international garrison at Pekin during the Boxer Rebellion in 1906. But what really impressed Mr Jones, during that episode Sub-Lieutenant Dew had met and spoken to "Mark Twain". Despite the pupils of Pinhoe School's incessant playground perusal of *Comic Cuts*, *The Beano* and Sexton Blake, they knew S.L. Clemens, or Mark Twain, well enough as the author of *Tom Sawyer*, whom every red-blooded boy liked to identify with, if not with the even more disreputable Huckleberry Finn.

Clemens had once been foreign correspondent for the *New York Times*, and in that capacity had been trapped in Pekin with the besieged forces, so it is possible that he and young Sub-Lieutenant Dew really had met.

As far as the children could see, Arthur Dew's more immediate claim to fame lay in his pleasing habit as a School Manager of treating the whole school, teachers included, of an annual visit to the pantomime at Exeter's Theatre Royal. He went as well, and chuckled and applauded as heartily as any one at the jokes and songs — which in those days were comparatively innocent. Afterwards the charabanc took him and his guests, still chattering excitedly, back to the little bridge outside his home where, prompted by their headmaster, they chorused "For He's a Jolly Good

Fellow" at the tops of their voices while the old gentleman paused in his lighted doorway to look back at them, hat raised in acknowledgement.

After thus voicing their appreciation on the way up Pinn Lane and Station Road there would be time for some of the older boys, inspired by the recent *entre-act* offerings of Buttons and his fellow comics in front of the pantomime curtain, to wind up their jollification with a kind of nonsense-announcement of the music hall master-of-ceremonies sort:

> Lay-dees — an' — gen'lemen —
> The nex' zong will be a dance
> Played by a vemale barry-tone
> Readin' a pome off of a one-stringed trumpet
> While zitting on the corner of a round table
> Drinkin' square oranges
> An' eatin' coconut vinegar off of a vork!

This was regarded by the participants as excruciatingly funny, and never failed to put the finishing touches to any enjoyable outing for them, if no one else. Then the passengers would be dropped off at The Corner under the watchful eye of their headmaster.

CHAPTER
THREE

Jobs and Geography

Nowhere in the same class as Arthur Dew, as regards his past activities and present benevolence, was another of the school managers, Mr John Brown. This John Brown was inevitably confused in the minds of young children with that other John Brown of American anti-slavery fame, whose name frequently cropped up in Mr Jones' school singing-lessons.

Mr Brown owned a horticultural nursery, market garden and orchard occupying part of the original Play Moor between the rear of Station Road (formerly Playmoor Lane) and the upper part of Langaton Lane, (an area now thoroughly denatured by a housing estate). A narrow side-entrance at the bend of Playmoor Gardens, which still runs behind Hazeldene and Westleigh and down behind the back gardens of Playmoor Villas, is all that remains of John Brown's nurseries; and even the high wooden door to that is missing. As well as providing the village with lettuces, tomatoes, cucumbers and several kinds of fruit, Mr Brown employed a number of Mr Jones's male school-leavers. The side door referred to was kept locked, and by seven o'clock on every work-day morning a half dozen or so youths gathered there, waiting for the sound of the brickworks' hooter from across the village, when John Brown's foreman would unlock the door from the inside and let them in.

THIS hooter might be compared to the air-raid warnings of a decade and a half later, except that like most mechanical devices of those days that were not horse powered, it was driven by steam. It had a considerable influence on the lives of others beside the humble worker in greenhouse, farm, field and the brickyard itself, for it fulfilled the functions of a communal alarm clock, alerting the entire village to the sad fact that another working day had begun.

The brickyard (a huge extension of it occupies more or less the same site today) stood halfway along Chancels Lane between Vinny Bridge, carrying the main road over the railway line, and Harrington Lane which then skirted the lower fringes of the Church Path Fields. These two large meadows, usually up for hay in summer, were bisected by a footpath leading down from the churchyard. Harrington Lane is now a suburban street. North of it, between its strip development and the ancient church and graveyard, the footpath has been diverted, fenced off around the rim of an enormous crater that resembles something in the Bad Lands of Dacota or Nebraska, the result of an impact from a comet, or an error in underground nuclear experiment. This is the latest clay-pit opened up by Pinhoe's up-dated hive of industry, Tarmac Bricks, and provides a bird's eye view of dinky-toy-like tractors and excavators hundreds of feet down, hauling and scraping at the bowels of poor old Pinhoe amid a litter of corrugated iron and coils of cable and pools of muddy water. Pinhoe bricks seem to be more in demand than ever. Rich purplish red, very hard and durable, much of post-war Exeter is built of them, and most of today's new Pinhoe.

It is difficult to believe now, peering down into the depths of that colossal muddy crater, or what you can see of it past the shoulders of the houses and bungalows in between, that half a century ago in early summer there were acres of sweet pollen-heavy hay in those Church Path Fields, soon to be cut by horse-drawn "windmill" mowers. What glorious hay-fights boys and girls waged over the ramparts they built out of the drying swathes, laughing and choking and sneezing as they threw handfuls of the stuff at each other, and in between times rolling about luxuriously in it! Yellowhammers and greenfinches, buntings and linnets called their monotonous notes from the leafy hedge-tops along Harrington Lane. Hurrying homewards at dusk, prickled and dusty and dry after all that heady-perfumed hay, you passed between low-lying fairy lanterns — the milky green luminescence of glow-worms hanging from the grasses and weeds alongside Harrington Lane. Half a dozen glow-worms on a tuft of moss in a jam-jar, and you could see to read your comic by them.

And the hayricks . . . they stood in the corners of almost every field. Built like solid cottages, they averaged about the same size and, like them, were thatched with straw. They made splendid places to shelter from wind and rain and were popular with tramps and courting couples, though of course what they were really for was winter feed for horses and cattle. To get hay from a rick someone would climb a short ladder, remove part of the thatch and with a large hay-knife on a curved wooden or iron handle, cut or saw out slabs of the compressed hay. Sometimes it was a sort of tread-knife not unlike a very broad-bladed and sharp edged garden spade. Such implements were made by the local blacksmith in sizes and shapes dictated by tradition, in other words as had been insisted on to the blacksmith's father or grandfather by some rustic expert half a century or more earlier. The hay was so closely compacted (and smelling very like perfumed tobacco) that it cut almost like cheese, and needed to be teased out and shaken loose before it could be fed to the animals.

A hayrick in a field was a most picturesque sight, included in many an artist's scene from rural life, very different to the hideous rolls of hay, wrapped in tattered black polythene sheeting and left lying in a field or piled into heaps anchored down with garlands of old motor tyres these days. But the modern procedure, with a machine that does the wrapping, leaves the farm worker more time for playing "vooter" and watching the telly, and horses no longer needed to do the work.

Other employers who obliged Mr Fred Jones by occasionally taking on some of his male school-leavers were Whippels of Exeter, and Garton & Kings, iron founders and stove manufacturers respectively. The

London & South Western Railway (after 1922 plain Southern) now and again took on a young fellow at and around the station at Pinhoe or at its sheds and depots at Exeter. Girls usually went into domestic service, or the brighter ones into offices in Exeter, or shops like Colsons or Bobby's or Waltons, all of whose various departments teemed with attractive young ladies.

The railway level-crossing that separated Station Road from Pinn Lane was a centre of adolescent attraction when a train was due, especially if one of the great *King Arthur* Class locomotives got held up by a signal-arm at "stop", and the locomotive itself stood champing and seething on the crossing while its god-like driver and fireman, their features desirably daubed with coal-dust and grease, winked companionably down from their cab at the little group of admirers on the other side of the high, closed crossing gates.

It was every red-blooded boy's ambition to be an engine-driver when he grew up, once he had given up hope of becoming a Red Indian. And no wonder! Those great green and brass and steel monsters with their squat stream-lined chimneys, steamy breaths and gleaming sweating flanks, thrusting connecting-rods and six-foot driving-wheels could never be thought of as mere inanimate machines. They had personalities of their own, wholly lacking in today's diesel zombies, with names to match: *Queen Guinevere*, *Sir Kay*, *Merlin*, and *King Arthur* himself. Their like will never been seen again . . . Normally they roared, whistling, straight through Pinhoe station, first stop Salisbury, at speeds of eighty miles an hour, with Waterloo to be reached dead on time as a matter of course.

There was a large and busy goods siding at Pinhoe Station, part of it given over to Bindon's coal-yard. The fathers of several boys at school were shunters or couplers there, with at least one driver for the hard-working little saddle-tank engine that did the shunting. One or two were signalmen operating the signals and points and the crossing gates from the glass-fronted signal-box. The crossing gates were in two pairs, with heavily wire-meshed white-painted timber frameworks, each with a vertical red-for-danger semi-sun that fitted against its neighbour to make a two-foot diameter warning disc, whether the gates were closed to road traffic or to trains. Iron chocks in the middle of the road on each side of the levelled-up double tracks were raised or lowered from the signal-box to prevent the gates swinging past their closed-to-the-road positions.

Boys loved to stand on these chocks as they went up or down. "Git off of them chocks!" the least tolerant of the signalmen would shout down at them from an open window, very much in the manner of Miss Barbara's groom. The gates themselves were operated by spinning a heavy black iron wheel round and round. That was another job a boy would not have minded doing.

There was a second siding half a mile farther down the line, on the Exeter side of Vinny Bridge and the hump-backed Chancel's Bridge, into Pinhoe Brickyard, with nearly always a string of open trucks waiting to be loaded, or tightly tarpaulin-covered, ready to be shunted out.

The Pinhoe signal-box, long since removed, along with those great pairs of double gates, has been preserved by a railway enthusiast, and stands now at Bere Alston on the old Tavistock (Great Western) line, still labelled with its Southern Railway Station name: Pinhoe.

Lost Whereabouts

The lay-out of today's Pinhoe is nothing like it used to be, extending far beyond its old boundaries. Former inhabitants, were they to be resurrected prematurely from among the crowded dead in the churchyard and return downhill towards what was once The Corner, might well conclude they had been misdirected by Old Nick and reached Purgatory instead. The lower part of Church Hill and its turning, now complete with traffic bollards in the middle, would be unrecognisable, the broad sweep into the formerly narrow Harrington Lane a startling change.

There used to be a wheelwright's workshop a little way along Harrington Lane, near the approach to the new school. The wheelwright's name was Pratt, not to be confused with the other Pratt, of the ethyl petrol dispensed by Henry Bindon from his hand-operated pump. Wheelwright Pratt's little girl Lucy went to the village school.

Cartwheels, whole waggons and their shafts, wheelbarrows, pickaxe handles: each was fashioned from its appropriate wood. A cartwheel was built up of apple-wood or hornbeam, ash, elm and oak, all hand-sawn and shaped and spoke-shaved and fitted together to be finally painted in traditional reds and blues and yellows.

Down in his smithy on the main road, almost opposite the Mission Church, Blacksmith Rogers would bellows-up his furnace and after a calculating glance at Mr Pratt's latest wheel would heat and bend an inch-thick strip of iron and weld it into a circle fractionally too small to fit around it. Meanwhile the wheelwright would carefully position his wheel on the huge circular, slightly convex stone slab, let into the ground at the entrance to the smithy, with a round hole in the centre to take the projecting hub. Then the two of them, each with a pair of long iron tongs, would carry out the red-hot iron tyre and drop it, smoking and sizzling, around the rim of the wheel, tap it gently into place with long-handled hammers and immediately throw buckets of water over it to douse and shrink it. Steamy smoke and the reek of charred wood, and felloes, spokes and hub all locked together; it was part of another arcane rustic art for the young to gather round and get in the way and gape at and argue over absorbedly.

Now, at the foot of Church Hill — if you can guess where its foot is — the age-old Corner has gone; obliterated, built over. Only the Poltimore Arms remains to provide a point of reference, and a railed pavement around it where no pavement or any kind of railings were before. The triangular turnpike house between the entrances to Station Road and Langaton Lane has gone. Long gone is the Coronation Seat (George V and Queen Mary, 1911), gift of Mrs Carr (who was Mrs Carr?) sheltering beneath the bramble-shaded overhang of the high hedge opposite the pub, where the old gaffers used to sit and smoke and spit and watch the little world of those days go by.

Nor is there that subsequent early concession to human "progress", RAC Road Scout Charlie Cotton, with his blue, grey and white motor-cycle combination parked at the roadside close by, on duty to regulate the burgeoning traffic of the 1920s: a pony and trap, a stately chauffeur-driven limousine, an Oxford-bagged articled auctioneer in his three-wheeled chain-drive Morgan, two ladies on push-bikes, a child on a scooter, a wandering dog.

Charlie Cotton was not altogether approved of by Headmaster Jones, thanks to his habit of smoking while on his traffic duties, and even more reprehensibly of passing on his discarded dog-ends to those of the village boys who hopefully hung around him. He had always meticulously saluted Headmaster Jones on the latter's way to and from school and addressed him as "Sir", until the latter's complaints about him reached official ears and were passed down to him, after which he equally meticulously refrained from saluting Headmaster Jones and calling him "Sir", but went on smoking while on traffic duty, just the same, and passing on his dog-ends to the same little gang of admiring hangers-on.

The present knot-work of white figure-of-eights denoting a "double roundabout" is surely never where Charlie Cotton used to stand to regulate the meagre traffic through irregular puffs of cigarette smoke! — In the evenings after he had ridden off on his motor-cycle combination, still with a fag stuck confidently between his lips, the youths of the village would gather to whistle and call out suggestive offers to the local young ladies teetering provocatively past on unaccustomed evening-wear high heels; or they would gather round an envied contemporary on his brand-new Norton or Triumph or Ariel (thirty bob down and half a guinea a week out of a wage of £2.10s.) with his "bird" dolled up for their evening out astride the pillion seat behind him until Nemesis or Priapus caught up with the pair of them, and the bike went back to the dealers and its former proud owner became a suddenly and reluctantly married man.

The triangular turnpike house had long abandoned its barrier pikes in favour of a sign inviting you to spend your toll money on a newspaper instead. But it was Freddy Pyle with his ambitious Corner Stores (Groceries and Provisions) established in the early 1930s, after the Coronation Seat was taken away, who really started Pinhoe's slide into urbanisation. Then, Loman the builder from Exeter, in competition with Tom Tapley, Builder & Undertaker, put up a row of houses in his field next to the school, which also helped. And another Freddy at the opposite side of The Corner — Freddy Patch's garage and filling-station — in a similar spirit of competitiveness, this time with

Henry Bindon . . . All three of them are gone now, though all three of them did well enough in their time, and all have left multiples of replacement memorials to their commercial ambitions, including a Bank.

The new post office — as distinct from the old one at Pound Cottage — is now itself an old one. It used to be in Station Road, when notices on its windows and outside walls exhorted you to use Robin Starch, eat Fry's chocolate and join the Royal Navy or the Marines. The Cottrell family ran the village post office from 1881 but now, one hundred and fifteen years later, Miss Betty Cottrell, the last of her line, has retired and the post office has moved. Her counters and walls were free of the usual diversionary clutter to be found in most sub-post offices — and indeed most main ones — where the dispensing of stamps and payments of pensions and posting of mail seem to be only secondary and minor considerations.

Related to the Cottrells were the Harrises. Ruth Harris was an attractive young widow, another relic from that infamous First World War. She lived with her three young sons in one of a short row of cottages opposite the post office, known as Rosemount Terrace. The youngest, Joe, long ago and much to his later embarrassment, won first prize in a Baby Beauty Show down at the Fair Field.

A few doors down from Ruth Harris's cottage was Tom Rudd's Dairy. There one could buy "meelko", butter and clotted cream. Before that, it had been Havill's the Butcher's, until Havill moved to a bigger shop in Exeter. In due course it became some sort of launderette, but its façade and distinctive flat-arched windows have remained surprisingly unaltered since its time as a butcher's.

Almost opposite the Dairy was Webber's Bakers & Confectioners, formerly owned and run by Percy Harris, before the war claimed him and widowed the mother of his three sons. The bakery stood a little way back from the road with a forecourt to accommodate the vans that brought sacks of flour and sugar for the bread and buns and cakes, and sometimes a lorry laden with sack-covered blocks of ice dripping in water all the way from the ice-factory at Exeter. The ice was not for the bread or the buns or the cakes, or even for the icing on the latter, but for the vanilla ice-cream that Bob Webber sold during the hot summer months. A block would be broken up into a large wooden tub and liberally sprinkled with sal ammoniac and rock salt to slow down its rate of thawing, and a large metal container, filled with the custard mixture he made with skimmed milk from Tom Rudd's Dairy opposite, would be partly sunk in it.

He kept this tub of ice-cream on the rough brick floor of the bakery just inside its broad open entrance, with the great iron doors of the hot, domed bread ovens steaming and sweating a little way in on the left. The village children gathering round for their cones and wafers found themselves breathing in lungfuls of hot crusty air from batches of freshly baked loaves and buns, and as often as not a few pungent whiffs of white-aproned Bob Webber's cigarette smoke. Like Charlie Cotton, he nearly always had a fag stuck in his mouth with an inch or so of ash hanging precariously at its tip, whether he was sweating at his flour-dusted bench inside the oven-hot bakery, mixing and rolling out dough and slapping it into tins, or crouching over his tub of pale yellow ice-cream at the scarcely cooler entrance.

This persistent smoking and its resultant droppings got him into trouble with the health authorities more than once, when cigarette ash, and once even a fag-end, were found inside his loaves. But if any ash dropped off into his pail of ice-cream, he would carefully lift it out with the edge of the wooden spoon he used for cones and wafers and immediately be besieged by clamorous juvenile customers, scandalised at the thought of those few specks of ice-cream being wasted: "Gi' us a lick o' that, Bob!" And the indulgent Bob would allow them to wipe it off the spoon with a grubby finger, ash and all.

Ice-cream cones and wafers were a penny or two pence each, according to size. His bread, buns, doughnuts and "fancy cakes" varied similarly. A two-pound "tinned" white loaf in those days cost 4d., quarters $7^1/2$ d. "Fancy cakes" coated with icing or chocolate or desiccated coconut, cream horns with a dab of jam and topped with real "clotted", butterflies, splits, etc., averaged 2d. or 3d. each. The fag-ends and ash came free.

Once a year on Christmas morning Bob Webber's great bread ovens fulfilled a gratifyingly festive function when egg-barren hens, obstreperous cockerels, a child's pet rabbit or pieces of fat pork or brisket, all of them too large for cottage paraffin stoves, would be brought down to the bakery ready trussed and larded, to be slipped into those roaring hot caverns at 3d. a time, while the heads of households who had brought them filled in the cooking time at the Poltimore Arms.

Further down Station Road a field on the right once belonged to the Whitton family of Oaklea House, which stood in the background. While Messrs Whitton & Laing of Exeter is still going strong, the field is a field no longer, but the site of another "estate" crammed shoulder to shoulder with splendid examples of cosy domestic retreats, some dating back to the 1930s. Playmoor Villas opposite date back to the 1830s, before the coming of the railway and the station at the bottom of Playmoor Lane, which caused the road to be renamed. But the map shows a blank space where Hazeldene and Westleigh were built later on at the upper end of that row of Villas.

Try somewhere else. Try Langaton Lane, which branches down from the former Corner between what was the old Turnpike House and the still extant Poltimore Arms. On second thoughts, don't bother. For you will search there in vain for signs of John Brown's hothouses and orchards, finding only more and more and more unlimited housing. Try Causey Lane, lower down on the right, where Denny's very first school friend and birds' nesting companion once lived. He could not live there now unless in a neat and tidy suburban semi-. His old home with its few smallholding acres, its chickens, ducks, pigs, orchard, and family cow — all are gone, all indistinguishably built over.

When you reach the point where Causey Lane joins the bottom of Station Road, don't bother to cross the present level-crossing — not even when it seems safe to do so: that is, when the International Frontier-type poles are raised and the red warning lights have ceased their frantic winking. For if you felt lost before, you will feel even more lost now. For Pinn Lane "that was" has suffered the most shocking changes in Pinhoe.

The turning to the right, which formerly led to the "down" platform of the railway station, now leads to the present sports ground and "vooter vield", through further development, over the Pinn Brook and back to the original Pinn Lane. But the first few yards down old Pinn Lane, with Brookfields on the left (the earlier and rather pretentiously named Marlborough House) looks much the same from the road. So does the old Baptist Chapel a few yards farther down, which was formerly the somewhat Hebraic sounding Tabernacle.

But just past the Chapel, now the United Reformed Church, "Slum" or Blackall Court has been much altered. Named after the bishop, curiously christened Offspring Blackall, who was founder of the Girls' Modern School at Exeter, this was a manorial farmyard alongside the Pinn Brook, scarcely changed since manorial times, even when used to house the homeless after the "Gurt Vire". Ancient cob walls have now been knocked down, red mediœval stones topped with brash quartzitic concrete, and the whole place spruced up beyond recognition.

Even worse has befallen Arthur Dew's nearby Monkerton Manor at the other side of the Brook, unsuspected home to fabulous collections of oriental curios and treasures, obliterated to make room for another half dozen dwellings, part of an area now known as Manor Gardens.

Opposite Monkerton Manor was a short unmade track leading to Pinhoe's Lawn Tennis Club. Here on summery afternoons and evenings in the 1920s and '30s would come gentlemen in straw boaters, striped blazers, white open-necked shirts, and long cream cricket flannels, usually in ordinary outdoor shoes, their white rubber-soled ones swinging by the laces from rackets clamped in their presses. Ladies wore long white cotton frocks, white cotton stockings and white canvas shoes, the younger ones with bandeaux round their hair in emulation of the Wimbledon Ladies Champion, Suzanne Englen.

They would toss up for partners, crank up the net and adjust its height (a racket held upright on the ground and another one widthways on top). Sharp cries of "No!", "Out!" or "Away!" would soon begin to punctuate the drowsy air (the term "Fault" not yet being in general use). "Game!", "Set!" and "*Match!*" would lead to tea with some of Mrs Fred Jones's bakestones (Welsh griddle scones) on the verandah outside the little wooden pavilion.

The few children who had come with their parents might be lent rackets, probably too heavy for them, and watched and advised from the tea-tables while they patted the green-stained balls to each other. Little

Joyce Havill (Havills, Butchers, of Exeter) used to serve quite well, under-arm of course, as befitted the ladies in those days, when young Denny as often as not failed to return her shots, which would equally frequently provoke the whimsical comment from the watchers on the verandah: "There's a hole in your racket!"

One side of the tennis club was skirted by the Pinn Brook, edged with tangles of brambles and stinging-nettles. Today the stream has been scoured and double-bridged, its kingfishers, moorhens and dragonflies gone like the tennis field itself, which is unrecognisably built over.

The developers have missed a chance here, assuming that they intended to enhance the area rather than create a kind of imitation sewage outfall between the two bridges. Early maps show a second stream, Pilton Brook, rising less than half a mile away and joining the Pinn at this point to form a pool. Such a pool, probably the original village pond, had it remained or been re-excavated, would be a greater attraction than what is there today.

Monkerton House (not to be confused with Monkerton Manor) looks reassuringly much as it did in its former occupant Colonel Holmes's days. So does its high-up roadside barn of cob and brick. In the late 1930s the latter became briefly the newly formed Scouts' HQ with Mr Steer the Scout-Master and, briefly, Denny as ASM.

Vincent's Monkerton Farm stands opposite, behind high cob walls, its lofty medieval-style double-gated yard entrance invariably closed against the new suburban encroachment outside. But although recently granted Grade Two listed status, that may mean nothing to the public authority which now owns it. Cob walls deteriorate notoriously easily and, as has frequently been demonstrated in this area, one has only to fail to maintain the cappings of slate or tile or thatch and the weather will soon do the rest. The penalties for allowing that sort of thing to happen are laughably trivial when compared to the profits to be made from replacing the resultant rubble with another half dozen, let alone fare more, desirable residences.

The present Old Barn in Tithe Barn Lane behind Monkerton House is not the barn that housed the local tithings five hundred years ago. This one could hardly have housed a waggonload of mangolds. The real tithe barn stood farther along the lane named after it, about on the line of the supposed secret underground passage connecting the monastic Monkerton Manor with the conventual Monkerton House. A relic of those monachal times was ploughed up in a nearby field about 170 years ago; until recently it was in the possession of the Sellick family but is now in Exeter's museum: part of the alabaster figure of an angel, probably from an altar screen or reredos hastily got rid of during the Dissolution.

Up Sandrock Hill from the corner of Tithe Barn Lane could once be found the high overhanging sandstone rock itself, riddled with tiny tunnels where sand martins nested year after year, their spring arrival promptly noted by the Causley brothers, who passed that way twice daily, to and from school. There is no longer any Rock, only a featureless and not very sandy slope to a corner of the field above, and certainly no sand martins.

Around the Rock to its left, Gypsy Hill was once a long country lane leading *via* Blackhorse Lane to Honiton Clyst but is now abruptly cut off just past the entrances to Gypsy Hill House. This was the former home of Colonel Chichester, then the O'Briens' Riding School and now a hotel. Pinhoe House opposite, an Old People's Home until about 1992, was then re-converted to private use. Danny would pause astride his bike outside the drive gateway of Gypsy Hill House to watch the Colonel practising his fly-fishing casts on a bit of white paper placed in the middle of his croquet lawn. The not unimposing house is now perched uncomfortably close to the edge of a broad deep cutting, which has sliced through Gypsy Hill to make room for the ever-intrusive M5, a frightening, rip-roaring hundred feet down.

Once only a short distance farther along Gypsy Hill Lane, but accessible today only by a very roundabout route, there stood until recently a splendid red brick mansion, Red Hayes.

Red Hayes, alas, had a very brief history. Built in 1895 by Arthur Walrond of bricks brought over from Holland to Topsham, and thence conveyed by horse-drawn wagons, the house was sold to Colonel Hext in 1905. He had been staying with the Chichesters at Gypsy Hill while looking for somewhere to live after leaving the Army. His eldest son, Lieutenant Thomas

Hext, was killed in World War One; the second son became the Major Hext who was involved in the conception and building of Pinhoe's American Hall — very necessary after the re-siting elsewhere in the village of Headmaster Jones's former school, which had served as the venue for village functions since the beginning of the century.

Having changed hands several times since Major Hext's death, its latest owners intended a grandiose future for Red Hayes and its ninety acres of parkland, only to suffer a couple of grievous setbacks; not only the destruction of the mansion itself by a fire of the same suspect origins as the one that had damaged the interior of Poltimore House, but then the highly questionable withholding of planning permission to replace it.

Also destroyed; or allowed to fall into disrepair, left to accommodate tramps and vandals, and now little better than a heap of rubble; was the lodge with stables and garage (the latter complete with workmanlike inspection pit) formerly occupied by Frederic Johns, the Colonel's (and Major's) chauffeur-groom. Young George Johns attended Pinhoe School, and a long-distance trudge and trot he had to make of it every weekday, part of it in company with the Causley brothers, whom he met with or parted from at the red stone Sand Rock.

But at least the whereabouts of the former Red Hayes and the remains of its lodge can still be seen.

Next to Gypsy Hill House or Hotel, running down beside it and almost opposite the rather gaunt red-bricked Pinhoe House, is a seldom used rough-surfaced lane, which connects the now abbreviated Gypsy Hill Lane with Tithe Barn Lane below. There used to be two cob and thatched cottages halfway down this lane, with a family called Gray living in one of them. "Sonny" Gray was about the same age as Howard, and the two of them often went birds'-nesting together in the Easter holidays. A cindery clearing opposite what used to be the Colonel's and then the O'Briens' stable yard probably marks the site of those two cottages.

At right-angles to Pinhoe House was a wing or annexe known as Endiang, which except for its name looks much the same today. Mrs Featherstone and her son Sam lived at Endiang. She was another of the village's many widows, her husband having inevitably been killed in the War. Mrs Featherstone's name greatly intrigued at least one youthful analytical mind — doubly so in relation to her probable weight. How well off or otherwise her husband may have left her was difficult to guess. She dressed eccentrically but fairly expensively in old-fashioned wide decorated hats, flowing capes, ribbons, and a multiplicity of skirts and wore a number of heavily jewelled rings on most of her fingers. However, she owned no motorcar and employed only one general servant, which put her as not much better off than the village headmaster. She spoke in a forced and husky voice, the folds of wattle round her neck and throat flapping and wobbling, and suffered very likely from some form of cancer.

Sam, who must have been rising thirty in the 1920s, was unmarried and unattached, except very commendably to his mother, and seemed to have no interest in the ladies. Mr Fred Jones's wife spoke of him somewhat whimsically as "a mother's boy", though he was generally accepted in the village as "a gentleman", that is "of leisure", occupying himself harmlessly if uselessly by driving about the countryside in his pony-trap and dropping off at pubs, or hunting with the Stoke Hill Beagles when he officiated as "cap", standing at open gateways and holding out that article of headgear beggar-wise to those of the hunt followers who filed in past him for the start of the day's fun. Sam was short-sighted and tended to stare straight through people he knew perfectly well, thus unintentionally but effectively "cutting them dead".

His mother was a great one for "visiting", especially round about tea-time. This was the tea-time of the idle rich and the pseudo-rich; mid-afternoon around three-thirty when the heads of the households were safely out of the way at their hunting or fishing or shooting or occupied with their nurseries, market-gardens, professions or estates, or in one instance not yet home from his school. Mrs Featherstone would cover a half mile or more to the village on foot, on her rounds of well-tested and approved hostesses, amongst whom, very sensibly, she included the headmaster's wife. Sometimes she called at two or three different houses the same afternoon, thus treating herself to a number of free teas.

The headmaster's wife was not always pleased to see her, not being a true member of the idle rich and usually at work at her cooking in the kitchen. But she would resignedly dust the flour from her hands and take off her apron and entertain Mrs Featherstone in the drawing-room behind a hastily brought-out best silver teapot and complementary hot-water kettle on its little tilting frame over a tiny spirit-lamp. There was also a cakestand stacked with home-made pastries and bakestones, which Mrs Featherstone greatly appreciated. She never failed to say so and, indeed, was not unaware of a caller's obligations. If the small son of the house came wandering into the drawing-room in hopeful quest of something special to eat, he would find she had brought him a present of some kind: a great glass marble every bit of two inches across with a fascinating interior of colourful twists and whorls, or perhaps a hedge-sparrow's or a swallow's egg wrapped in cotton wool in a matchbox which she told him "her Sam" had given her to give him.

But back to Gypsy Hill House and sharp left down Gypsy Lane, named after those happy itinerants with their fairy-tale tree-houses on wheels drawn by piebald ponies, with baskets of split-stick clothes-pegs, stolen daffodils and "lucky" white heather, who sometimes camped in the adjoining field.

This field, although its slope faces north, has now become the Sandrock Wholesale Nurseries, created in a worthy move to replace the two or three local nurseries destroyed by the planners.

Thence down Gypsy Lane itself, on foot unless cautiously on horseback because of its uneven surface and overgrown hedges, gratifyingly even more neglected than seventy years back, and then into Tithe Barn Lane again, almost opposite the non-tithe barn. There, if you must turn right instead of left back towards Monkerton, brace yourself for a further rash of new housing and then for the dizzy fly-over which spans the motorway gashed through Major Hext's old land on the north side of Gypsy Lane, where mushrooms used to crop up overnight in autumn like light sprinklings of early snow, and rabbits paused, wrinkling their noses and pricking their ears, alert for prowling foxes.

At the end of this sadly suburbanised Tithe Barn Lane is a modest four-crossway, which still has an area of weed-grown allotment on the right, refreshingly not very much changed. But the village football field is no longer a few yards down Mill Lane opposite, having been resited in a field by the railway station where these days, alas, there are few waiting passengers able to benefit from that grandstand position on Saturday afternoons.

Down to the left from the cross-roads, in what is really the far end of Lower Langaton Lane, there is a little triangular field that once contained an ancient sweet-water spring, last made full use of during the Second World War when supplies of tap-water failed in the village because of the bombing. The spring bubbled up beneath a small archway under a tile-roofed linhay built over the flagstones that covered the well itself. Children used to lie face down in the buttercups and water-parsnips and cress, getting thoroughly soaked up their arms and down their fronts while cupping handfuls of crystal-clear water and gulping it down.

The linhay used to provide shelter for Pinhoe's personal "gentleman of the road", Oliver Jennings. The spring was known as Almon's or Elmon's Well. Local renderings of words, especially place-names, had hardly improved since Daniel Defoe commented on them during his journeyings through the Westcountry in the 1700s, so there was doubt as to what some words really were unless one saw them in print. But Almon's, Elmon's or Orman's Well, or variations of the name, was a catch-phrase among the youth of the village half a century ago, and the literal source for the quenching of many a juvenile thirst. Children, and not only children, frequently refreshed themselves at Almond's Well.

But however the name was pronounced or mispronounced and however historically pleasing if it could be attributed to some obscure local saint, as were so many wells, holy or otherwise, (St Alman, St Alban, St Olam?), it was probably named after the decidedly un-saintly Duke of Ormonde. He was once Lord Lieutenant and High Steward of Exeter, until his escape to France with his fellow Jacobite Viscount Bolingbroke after the failure of the Old Pretender's bid for the throne on the death of Queen Anne. He had owned the original house on Gypsy Hill, on the site of the much more recent Red Hayes, to which a water supply had been raised from this well by a horse-operated pump.

That, of course, was a long time ago. There was never any pump there, horse-operated or otherwise, in living memory. Now the gate leading to where it used to be is heavily barbed-wired. Not that anyone would want to go there today where one can hardly believe in the presence of a spring of water, bubbling up from the little arched side of a well. Excavations for the motorway into and through the side of Gypsy Hill entailed the removal of thousands of tons of soil and destroyed the water-table which until then had dipped north-east to supply the spring. One of the trigger-happy farming fraternity, never to be confused with the indulgent Farmer Hodge, added a final blow to that act of incidental vandalism by removing all traces of the linhay covering the well and of the well itself. Now there are only dense tangles of stinging nettles filling a dry ditch. No open-fronted linhay. No well beneath its hay-covered stone-flagged floor. No sign of any bubbling spring. No little shoals of minnows so delicately transparent you could see their tiny ribs and backbones through their skins as they darted about in the clear sandy shallows, where a cress-lined thread of crystal-clear water joined the Pinn Brook. And certainly no Oliver Jennings.

Instead, on the far side of that same field there squats a huge double-ended building (of Pinhoe brick, no doubt) its purpose revealed by a high mound of earth at a range of twenty-five metres from its inner end. So featureless and obviously functional is this monstrosity, it ought surely to be a modern "industrial" agricultural building of some kind. In fact it represents the village's compensation for its lack of any historical archery butts. Whatever the population of Pinhoe or Pennoc or Pinnoo may have contributed to its country's defence in the Middle Ages, presumably it was not skilled longbow men. Gone now are the inveterate birds' nesters and tree climbers and "muckers about" who habitually trespassed in those fields with wonky muzzle-loading Daisy airguns, firing bits of grit at anything that moved but preferably did not (not for them the use of "proper" .177 round shot, which had to be "boughten"). But their sons may be practising their more sophisticated skills against cardboard "bulls" with Anschutz or BSA "target" .22s.

The Village Tramp and Fred Gee

How times and names have changed! And, also, the sort of people one might chance to encounter in what is now left of those country lanes.

Howard had a story to tell about that embarrassing name-sake of the vicar, the village tramp, Oliver Jennings. He "stunk like an ol' fox" according to local legend, though his occasional occupation of the linhay at Ormonde's Well in a nest of damp straw, old coats and mouldy sacking apparently caused no pollution of its waters.

Young Howard at the age of eight or nine had been wandering by himself in the region of Blackhorse Lane, halfway towards Honiton Clyst, and had got himself lost. Providentially, along came Oliver Jennings, draped as usual in three or four overcoats, worn summer or winter, and hung about with numerous bags and bundles and strings of old tins and empty bottles. "Arternoon, sonny," Oliver greeted him, and would have passed by. Howard, more worried about being lost than by Oliver Jennings's looks and uncertain reputation, piped up politely, "Please sir, can you tell me where I am? I'm lost." Intrigued no doubt by this unusually courteous greeting, "Where do 'ee come from, Sonny?" the tramp enquired, adding "You come along of me, then," when Howard had told him. So forth went tramp and village headmaster's son till they reached the gate into Ormonde's Well, where Oliver was currently pigging it in the linhay over his permanent water supply. Knowing then where he was, Howard said "Thank you very much, sir," and ran off home.

He chuckled over this minor adventure in after years, emphasising the harmlessness of Pinhoe's local vagrant.

Oliver was reputed to be an old soldier left over from the last war, and like so many of those jobless former saviours of their country, had opted for the vagrant's peacetime way of life. If little boys or little girls, seeing him in the distance, tended to hide or run away they need not have worried. Oliver's weaknesses were for other people's rabbits and pheasants and even sheep, which he would dispose of to an uninquisitive butcher of his acquaintance. But he never wandered very far from the village where he had become pretty well known, and where he could usually be sure of a crust and a lump of cake and a mug of tea at doors such as Mrs Jones's.

But as winter approached and conditions in the linhay deteriorated in spite of additional deposits of moth-eaten rags and mouldy hay, Oliver would go to great lengths to get himself caught red-handed by PC Holman and sent up before the "beak", to spend the winter in a nice warm prison cell with food and exercise free. Or he would give himself up after breaking a few windows, with the same objective in mind. It meant he would have to have a bath and endure the attentions of the prison barber; but that presumably was a small price to pay for a few months out of the cold and wet.

Denny experienced a not dissimilar encounter several years later, not with Oliver Jennings, but in an episode with an equally tame anti-climax.

One of his father's rare scholastic failures had some years earlier made his escape from that gentleman's pedagogic care so shortly before the minimum school-leaving age of fourteen that it hardly mattered. (Apocryphally, it had followed an abortive punishment when he had snatched the cane from his headmaster's hand, snapped it in two and flung the pieces back at him and run off, never to return.) Thence he had graduated almost at once to the Reformatory School near Whipton, and thereafter as soon as he came of age, as it were, was in and out of Exeter gaol with predictable regularity. His name, no less embarrassing for Mr Fred Jones than Oliver Jennings's was for the Reverend Oliver Puckridge, was Fred: Fred Gee. He was a by-word in the village for blatant disreputableness, but was not altogether unadmired by its more irresponsible elements. PC Holman's curiosity was frequently aroused by the worry of what he might be up to. He was reminiscent of such reprobates as Gray's "little tyrant of the fields" and Masefield's Saul Kane, but history does not record if he ever experienced the latter's spiritual redemption.

Denny, at any rate, had been wandering along that same part of Langaton Lane past Ormonde's Well when who should he see striding jauntily towards him but Fred Gee, attired almost unrecognisably in neat shiny blue suit and black bowler hat. A sardonic grin appeared on his face as he recognised the young son of his hated former headmaster. His greeting sounded none the less harmless enough. "Wot you got there, then, Denny?" Denny had just picked a dried-up oak-apple with the intention of adding it to what he was pleased to think of as his natural history collection, which consisted largely of birds' eggs. "It's an oak-apple" he informed the other instructively. Everyone knew Fred Gee had been the prime dunce of the school during his time there, only excelled since by his successor Nasty. "Garn. That's not an oak-apple. That's an oak-*gall*."

The word was unfamiliar to the boy. But to be corrected or contradicted by Fred Gee was unthinkable. Only too conscious of his superior status as "skulemaizder's zun" he stuck to his guns. "No it isn't. It's an oak-*apple*".

"It's an oak-*gall*," grinned Fred Gee. "There's a little insec' inside it."

This was even more intolerable. "No, there isn't."

"'Ere — give it 'ere —" Fred Gee drew an enormous clasp knife out of his pocket and far from murdering little Denny with it, in a moment had sliced his oak-apple in half. "There y'are wot did I tell 'ee?"

Denny gazed in wondering discomfiture at the tiny curled-up proof of Fred Gee's unaccountable genius.

"That's zummat yer know-all skulemaizder vaither never told 'ee," commented Fred Gee; and he tilted his bowler hat over one eye and strode off, highly pleased with himself.

Fred Gee lived with his widowed mother (another consequence of the recent War) in one of the cottages in Southleigh Terrace beside the main road, uncomfortably close to the police house occupied by PC Holman. On this occasion he had been on his way to visit a lady friend at Honiton Clyst, in celebration of one of his rare visits to the outside world, which accounted for his shiny suit and bowler hat and generally spruced-up appearance.

Denny did not mention this encounter to his parents, with the unacceptable inference that Fred Gee knew anything at all, other than how to keep getting himself sent to prison, let alone something that Denny himself (and dare one suggest it, possibly even his father) did not know.

The Reformatory School, Fred Gee's intermediate *alma mater*, featured briefly at least once in the lives of some of Mr Jones's senior boys, but not with a promise of possible joys to come once they had escaped from his charge. Only Nasty was destined to follow in Fred Gee's reprehensible footsteps, though because of the hold-up in his classroom progress he was debarred from this trial visit to the place.

One hot day in early July a small party of boys set off from the school playground, swimming costumes and towels rolled up under their arms, with Mr Fred Jones in charge, a stern-eyed but indulgent shepherd among a not wholly trustworthy flock of sheep. Along the main road they trooped, all the way up Church Hill, past Lady Hull's Beacon Down House, past the site of the Beacon itself, Cheyney Gate and the little lane opposite that led down to Danes' Wood, past Goffin's Farm (whence Ruby Westaway and her brother, a second Raymond, would later be coming to Pinhoe School), then a further half mile to the four-lane junction at Stoke Post, to turn left past Silverton Kennels and walk almost halfway to Pennsylvania at the Old Tiverton Road end of Exeter. There, at a red-bricked edifice on the left, adapted for use as the district's Reformatory School for delinquent boys, Headmaster Jones led the way through the entrance. And there indeed they were — hot, tired and dusty and greatly in need of a bath or a bathe.

Official policies regarding such institutions of the minor corrective kind were aimed at making them agreeable, on the Owenian theory that social unfortunates, misfits and amateur criminals would emerge at the end of their period of detention "reformed", having responded agreeably to agreeable conditions. It wasa policy, which, much as today, was hardly conducive to discouraging wrong-doing. Apart from three good meals a day and far more comfortable surroundings than most of the inmates would have known in their own homes, they enjoyed all manner of extras which they would not have enjoyed in the outside world: properly laid-out football pitches and real footballs, cinema picture shows, gardening, a couple of gramophones, a gymnasium, the mixed blessings of "educational classes" and the unheard-of luxury of a swimming bath.

Swimming baths, as they were commonly called in those days, were comparatively rare phenomena in the country. Nearly every town possessed its municipal swimming bath, it was true (the one at Exeter was in Gandy Street), and were usually juxtaposed with the public ablutionary baths. But few of even the most élite private houses had swimming-pools in their gardens or grounds, though they might have lily-ponds, boating and fishing lakes or rivers in which the men and children might sometimes bathe.

But here in the Reformatory School's great white-tiled swimming-bath the water looked invitingly green and cool. There was a diving-board and a long open-fronted shed for undressing in. The Pinhoe boys looked around them in awed wonder. They couldn't have been more impressed by a visit to Buckingham Palace.

The natural possessors of all that ill-deserved splendour were nowhere to be seen, much to the private relief of the visitors. The notorious Fred Gee was one of the inmates, and might well have welcomed his former headmaster and his bunch of namby-pampy law-abiding schoolboys by pulling faces and making rude noises at them.

The Pinhoe boys splashed and wallowed rumbustiously but were under strict orders not to try any horse-play. Mr Jones himself, in full-length swimming costume of black embarrassingly dropsical-sagging cotton, showed off his trudgen-stroke to admiring pupils. Few of the latter could actually swim, though some manfully tried to, helped and encouraged by a headmasterly hand under their chins.

Mr Jones had been able to effect this pleasing diversion after correspondence with the school's principal or headmaster on the subject of Fred Gee's qualifications for admission.

Sometimes down in the village, usually on a Sunday afternoon, the entire complement of the Reformatory School was to be seen shambling along the lanes on a routine exercise outing, in drab travesty of a girls' school crocodile, in the charge of two or three harassed-looking masters. A shabby, grinning, untrustworthy lot they looked too, guaranteed to strike awe if not genuine terror to the heart, and deter latent lawless ambitions among the Pinhoe young.

Albany Evered Payne

If Pinhoe could claim few other individualists of the calibre of the Reverend Oliver Puckridge and Oliver Jennings, at least it had Albany Evered Payne halfway between them.

Albany Evered Payne had left Pinhoe School by 1926 at the usual age of fourteen (until when, of course, much fun had been got out of his middle name), with no particular skill unless it was at gardening.

Never having been a troublesome pupil, and with his headmaster's recommendation, he had no difficulty in finding full employment, if only at helping to grow lettuces and tomatoes at Mr John Brown's nursery.

But even full employment implies time off.

In the hedge bordering the Pinn Brook along the left hand side of the Ormonde's Well field and a good fifty years before the rifle range was put up, there used to be a tall lightning-blasted tree, an elm or an alder, leafless and all but barkless, rearing high above its surroundings. A few large boughs still stuck out from its naked trunk, and near its summit a part of it had broken off to leave a large niche or hollow some sixty feet or so above the ground. On alternate Saturday afternoons when Pinhoe's football team was playing away, and provided the weather was not too wet or cold, a figure was to be seen seated comfortably in this hollow, legs stretched out along one of the nearest dead branches. It was Albany Evered Payne up there, reading a book.

Mr Jones might have been mildly gratified and surprised that Albany troubled to read at all, never mind climbed some sixty perilous feet up a dead tree to do so. But perhaps Albany Evered felt a need for seclusion to counter the frequent flippant inquiries prompted by his middle name. What books he read, there is no knowing: only blood-and-thunders, perhaps, but never mind.

Now Albany Evered lies six foot underground in Pinhoe churchyard, instead of reclining sixty feet up in Pinhoe air, and never again will anyone pull his leg with "Ever read so-and-so, Albany?"

More Used to Was-es!

Along the rest of Langaton Lane, back towards this village "as used to was", there is worse than the extinction of Ormonde's water-cressed well and the loss of the dead tree where Albany Evered Payne used to perch reading his books. The little timber-railed water-bridge over the Pinn looks much the same as it always did though the rails themselves, still scratched and incised with rustic symbols, including hearts-and-arrows and Denny's initials, are now in need of replacement. The track through the gateway beside the bridge once ran alongside the Pinn, across several fields to the banks of the River Clyst, and thence to the Mill at the lower end of Mill Lane, but now only its first few hundred yards remain.

The route taken by boys going minnowing or farther afield to the river for swimming or fishing half a century ago was through that same gateway and across those same fields, but where no sign of a track was discernable. Possibly a lingering atavistic memory shared by their contemporaries kept them to it: their fathers or grandfathers had always gone that way. The much longer route along Mill Lane was seldom attempted except by those with bicycles. The only other route was a rather over-exciting one along the railway line; of which more anon.

Today the view from that water bridge is no longer towards the delectable-sounding sewage farm or "zooje varm", another place to trespass, among highly unaromatic open settling-tanks and sewery osier-beds, in order to peep in at the green-painted steel and brass pumping-engine housed in its little brick building. The sewage works were not there before the early 1900s. The sewage disposal system in most places in the village before then were modest little structures at the far ends of every garden, as shown on the map of 1889, except in the case of Playmoor Villas. The latter would have been built with indoor WCs, first thought of in the 1770s but not in general use for another fifty years, with cess-pits in the gardens or not far away. Neither method was nearly so inefficient in the long run as "modern drainage". Earth-loos and cess-pits needed to be emptied every now and again, and the contents distributed by conservation-minded gardeners over fruit and vegetable plots. But the resultant legacy of "rich fertile soil" is often quoted in today's house-sales literature in respect of old country cottages and their gardens, though the reason for that richness and fertility is not often mentioned.

Most of those cottages had wells for drinking-water, the inference of contamination being obvious but by no means correct. Garden soil and its micro-organisms are most efficient filters of bacteria, which is more than can be said of many of today's elaborate and expensive sewage disposal systems that discharge dubious effluents into streams and rivers and sea. There was no general pollution of rivers and beaches and sea until the ultra-hygienic water-closet got linked up to main drainage, and automatic washing-machines and detergents were invented.

Now, instead of Pinhoe's old sewage farm and its unforgettable effluvia, a bungalow stands in what used to be the adjoining "stoggy meadow", where small boys played at Red Indians among ragged tufts of rushes and scatterings of pale mauve ladies' smocks (or milkmaids), and the iron horses of the London & South Western Railway chugged past on their high embankment. There is a Scout Hut, too, on the other side of the lane, of the same design and materials as the rifle range, a long way from Miss Barbara's Wolf Cubs' lair at Beacon Down, though anything but a long way from the ubiquitous and never silent M5. The latter's lofty embankment dominates both the Scout Hut and the old embanked railway line and its little flat-arched bridge over Langaton Lane. This part of the lane is still recognisable, if you stand with your back to poor Robin's Hideaway and look in the opposite direction. Originally there would have been only fields and hedges to hide from, but now it is hidden more than originally intended, squashed between the unobtrusive sandstone bridge and the huge brash concrete span of the motorway.

The poor little cottage on the farther side, once the home of d'Arcy Ford, amateur song-writer, and his wife May, amateur singer, was once distinguished by a great Chilean pine in its little old world garden. Monkey Puzzle Cottage, it was generally called by the village children. It is one of the oldest houses still left in Pinhoe, dating from the late 1400s, when it served the monks of Monkerton as a guest house. Pity its occupants now, with that high concrete anachronism tight up against it!

A little farther up on the right there used to be a brick-backed horse-trough set into the hedge and fed through a lead pipe from a spring in the field behind. Opposite it in the broad grass verge lay the remains of a millstone brought up from Pinn Mill, broken and misshapen, with weeds growing out of its central hole. Neither of these minor local features remains, bulldozed away in the pursuit of suburban expansion.

A few more yards along on the left stood the cottage and outbuildings of Ash Farm, owned by a farmer appropriately named Hodge, symbolic term for rustics ever since Charles Kingsley coined it sixty years earlier. In the tiny front garden of Farmer Hodge's cottage stood a low brick well-head and beside it an iron pump, fitted with a long curved handle. Boys homeward bound from their favourite resort "round Zooje Varm" would knock at the door of this cottage and beg for a drink of water from the "missus" who opened it. Boys those days got as thirsty as stoats or weasels, or imagined they did, despite probably having sampled the water from Ormonde's Well not long before.

Farmer Hodge's missus frequently suffered such visitations, and with admirable forbearance would tell the little pests to help themselves and shut the door on them. Then they would work the great handle up and down, and presently ice-cold water would gush out from the iron spout into each upturned mouth in turn. It tasted vaguely of earth and moss, different from but no better or worse than what came bubbling up out of the arched aperture at the side of that other well.

Opposite Ash Farm stood a high rambling barn, belonging not to the easy-going Farmer Hodge but to one of his less amiable contemporaries, who had an unpleasant tendency to let off his twelve-bore (specially loaded with split peas instead of lead shot) at boys he caught trespassing on his land. Boys thus ran a bit of a risk when investigating the barn, which was always good for swallows' and house-martins' nests in the rafters, with who knew what other sorts tucked away in the crannies in the cob walls.

Near the junction of Langaton Lane with Causey Lane higher up, there still stands a solitary old-style cottage with another well and pump. Or at least, it used to be solitary, and it used to have a well and a pump. The O'Connors and their two daughters lived there in the 1920s and '30s, and after them a family called Griffin, the cottage walls by that time window-deep in late twentieth century brick and tile and glass divided by neat driveways of tarmac and concrete. Before that, there were only wide verges of grass, nettles and docks (the antidote to nettle stings) and *milky diashels* (dandelions or "rabbits' meat") backed by high hedge-banks topped with brambles, hazels and "bread-and-cheese" hawthorn — havens for innumerable small birds.

Now all that has gone as though it had never been. Now there are only houses and more houses, and side-roads between them lined with yet more houses. Where do all the people who live in them come from? And this is only a microcosm of what is happening everywhere. And where do all the hedge-sparrows and finches and warblers and long-tailed tits go to nest these days?

In late autumn and early spring came hedgers and ditchers along this lane, the hedgers sickling out unwanted weeds, "steeping" the soil, and laying the hazels and hawthorns with upward half-cuts of a pach-hook, then pleaching and pegging down the partly cut stems to grow into tight living fence-works. Ditches were scooped out in neat trenches ready for the winter rains. About the only tool used for this was the long bent-helved heart-shaped "Devon spade", a most unhandy-looking implement seemingly wholly unsuitable for the job. Yet everywhere was neat and tidy after the hedgers and ditchers had been at work — very different from the raw slashed chewed-up tatterings left by today's tractor-driven gashers and flailers.

Ditchers occasionally did duty as drainers, trenching and laying the plain clay drain-pipes end to end under nearby fields to drain into their newly cleaned-out ditches.

About once a year a Foden steam lorry would dump a load of road-mending rock on one of those grassy verges to be followed in a day or so by a stone-breaker, whose name was Rose. In collarless ex-army khaki shirt, corduroy trousers yorked round under the knees with leather straps to keep out crawling creatures, and heavy hobnailed boots, "Stony Rose", as the boys called him, sat on a bit of old sacking on top of his rocks and chipped away with a small heavy hammer, his eyes protected by an old pair of motoring goggles.

Day after day he sat happily at the same place, breaking up his pile of rocks into finished road-metal, all much of a size, gradually building up a raised platform with steep sloping sides and a dead level top; all done by eye, a painstaking labour of hardly less devotion and skill than that of the hedgers and ditchers.

For his midday dinners Stony Rose brought a few crusts of bread and a lump of cheese and a raw or pickled onion, to be washed down with mouthfuls of vinegary scrumpy from a small half-gallon cask (virkin), without benefit of mug or tankard.

Sometimes on their way up or down the lane, if they happened to catch him at his midday meal, those irrepressible bibbers of Adam's ale from spring or iron pump would beg him for a "zup o' yer zider, Stony!" by way of a change. — "Chikky young buggers! doan' 'ee take too much, now!"

The bung-hole would be hygienically wiped with a grubby palm. But the rough stuff was well nigh undrinkable to juvenile tastes, besides usually being strongly flavoured with onion.

Cider

Stony Rose's virkin of cider might have come from almost anywhere, so much of that beverage was made at farms and local cideries in those days. Farmer Hodge had a cider press in one of his barns and Stanley and Denny, two of his wife's pump-water nuisances, usually succeeded in hanging around when the press was about to be put into operation. Cartloads of astringent crimson-skinned "Stretch-me-Girdle" apples would be brought in from where they had been piled up under the trees in the orchards. Half of them would be rotten and crawling with inebriated wasps, and riddled with earwigs, comatose slugs, and might include the occasional remains of a dead rat. The whole lot would be sent on its journey of conversion into the traditional wine of Devon.

The apples were tipped out, just as they were, into a great wooden hopper, which fed them down to a pair of granite rollers, two pairs of juvenile hands being eager to turn the heavy iron cranks. The resultant *crush* was shovelled and patted into cheeses of tight-packed sacking and criss-crossed layers of wheat straw, and then the press in its clumsy timber framework, like an outsize printing-press left over from the Caxton era, was lowered on the cheese and screwed slowly down. This screwing-down process was a slow and leisurely affair, with a four-foot block of cheese to be pressed and trimmed and opened up for the loose dripping ends to be turned in and pressed again and again by Farmer Hodge and his carter Jim, one at each end of the heavy turn-bar. It could never be done all at once or even in a single day.

The pomace which drained out into a wooden trough at the base of the press was surprisingly sweet and syrupy, considering the unacceptably sour little apples that had gone into the crush and the variety of animal matter with them, which, however, would have greatly enriched the final brew. The pomace was racked off into huge oak hogsheads twice the height of a boy and ten times his girth. Fermentation took a matter of months, filling Farmer Hodge's barn with potent alcoholic odours so that the swallows and house-martins that nested high up in the rafters flew somewhat unsteadily in and out.

Farmer Hodge and Stanley's father were old friends, which perhaps explains the apple-crushing privileges enjoyed at Ash Farm by the two boys.

The present residential area called Ash Close covers the approximate site of Ash Farm and Farmer Hodge's cottage and outbuildings and aromatic barns; a few of his apple trees seem to have survived in some of the gardens.

Other Topographical Considerations

Causey Lane which starts (or ends) near the place where Stony Rose used to sit chipping at his rocks, drinking his scrumpy and erecting his temporary altar to the road-mender's art, is properly speaking Causeway Lane, Causey being a local rendering.

An uncertain thread of water occasionally seeped up from a boggy top corner of Loman's Field next to Mr Jones's school and was briefly visible beneath the old gaffers' spittoon grating beside the Coronation Seat at The Corner (it had dried up when Pinhoe's Fire Brigade stood most in need of it). Before the days of culverts and macadam, it had trickled openly across a dip in the turn-pike road, to run through that part of Play Moor which later became John Brown's nurseries and orchards, reappearing briefly from a drain halfway down Causey Lane, and finally joining the Pinn Brook behind Blackall Court.

It seems unlikely that this sporadic little stream could ever have flooded to such an extent that it necessitated the construction of a causeway. More probably there was a raised causeway lower down across the low flat area to the south and east, which might well have been flooded by the Pinn Brook after long spells of wet weather. This became known as Brook Field (giving its name to its owner's residence nearby, the former Marlborough House) and then the Fair Field, and was later used as the Flower Show Field. Built by the monks from Monkerton, a causeway here would have connected with their guest house in Lower Langaton Lane, the future Monkey Puzzle Cottage. The Yeovil & Exeter Branch Line passed very close to this cottage (as indeed the no-longer British Rail still does), and could well have been laid along the foundations of the causeway.

Two terraces of houses that were not built till after 1890, twenty years after the railway line first went past, are now too mixed up with 1990s additions to help clarify the issue. The original back-to-back terraces face in opposite directions, their back gardens separated by a narrow access alley. One faces the present railway and the former Brook Field and is named not very suitably Fairview Terrace: Fair*field* would have been more apt. The other, alongside Causey Lane, is Pinbrook Terrace: surely a misnomer. No one could possibly have confused the uncertain little rivulet from Loman's Field with the admittedly not much larger but indisputably more permanent Pinn Brook a good quarter mile away, on the other side of the railway line and running through the middle of the old Fair Field.

Although the 1801 map shows what might be traces of an original causeway connecting Monkerton with its guest house, some maps of the area are delightfully non-committal, while others have wild inaccuracies and omissions, except perhaps in the matter of Pinhoe's apparent plenitude of pumps and wells, which suggest an ever accessible water-table.

From Topsham to Clyst William, about thirteen miles to the north of Pinhoe, extends the complex and highly flood-prone Clyst Vale. Time was when ground would have lain under water after prolonged rain or in wet winters, from the lowermost part of Pinhoe and the Clyst's tiny tributary the Pinn Brook to the area further north around the former Broadclyst Station, where the B3185 road is still provided with flood-relief "dips" and, truly, a raised causeway.

In similar conditions the whole of the Clyst Valley from its source at Clyst William through Clyst Hydon, Clyst St Lawrence, Broadclyst, Clyst St Mary and Clyst St George to its estuary at Topsham would flood to a depth of several muddy feet. It still does today, despite various elaborate attempts to obviate what in fact was quite a boon to riparian landowners, revitalising their meadows with free deposits of fertile silt. At such times Broadclyst well deserved its name, and the Pinn became half a mile wide instead of its more usual modest few feet.

The vicinity of Causey and Langaton Lanes would certainly have needed a causeway. Monkey Puzzle

Cottage itself is set a little higher than the level of the lane in front of it and but for a raised causeway connecting with it from behind would have stood like a tiny island amid a vast inland sea after prolonged periods of rain, very much as the ruins of Pinn Mill near Honiton Clyst do today.

Stoggy Meadow, next to the former sewage farm, must have been one of the last areas to emerge from those once regularly inundated acres, helped no doubt by the construction of the railway embankment. The rest of the meandering Clyst Valley continues to uphold its time-honoured tradition of flooding almost every winter.

A rather better authenticated topographical feature than the causeway, with no less authentic historical connections marked on most maps of the area, is the one that gives its name to the height of land behind and above Pinhoe Church.

The earliest record of a beacon on what became known as Beacon Down dates from about AD 880, when one was sited there by Alfred the Great as part of his defence system against the Danes. Whether it was put to use before the Battle of Pinhoe a hundred years or so afterwards is open to question. The battle itself took place in the neighbourhood; that we do know.

In those days there would have been no intervening clump of woodland in the grounds of Beacon Down House, and the beacon would have been visible from the Exe estuary and the sea beyond, and across to other beacons on Woodbury, Haldon, Sidbury and the

Blackdown Hills. A Roman signal station had been established some two miles to the west of Beacon Down, which would also have commanded a better view then than now. But that had been six or seven centuries earlier.

It was not on the direct (if zig-zag) chain of fire beacons that reached from Plymouth to the roof of the old Admiralty building at Whitehall. Their flickering warning, as one after another was lit all the way along the coastline to Dover and beyond, was wryly remarked on by Admiral Medina Sidonia, when commanding the ill-fated Armada on its way up-channel. But it was very likely lit on the same occasion to relay the warning northwards. It also may or may not have served a similar function during the Napoleonic Wars, either as a fire-and-smoke signal beacon or as a site for one of the new-fangled semaphore telegraphs.

Denny was taken up to Beacon Down as a child and shown a twisted and rusted framework of iron girders sticking out of the ground. In his innocence, he believed he was looking at the remnant of a Saxon beacon or at least a Napoleonic one. In fact it was the left-over cage-work from a huge communal bonfire (still a beacon fire of a kind) dating from November 1918 to celebrate the end of the First World War.

The huge increase in housing in the neighbourhood and expansion of the population, with the consequent increase of the consumption of water, led to the construction of a reservoir on the site of Pinhoe's historic Beacon, effectively putting paid to the prospect of any 1995 VE anniversary bonfire being lit on that spot. Not that Pinhoe would have had much to celebrate, seeing that the end of the war began the end of Pinhoe as a village.

CHAPTER
FOUR

Juvenile Joys

Mention has already been made of wild birds and their nests. During springtime and early summer, and not limited to the Easter and Whitsun holidays, birds' nesting was almost a major industry among the young males of the village. There were few of them who did not add to or wantonly duplicate their modest collections year after year. Most did so without any genuine interest or knowledge of the subject, blowing the eggs through ragged pin-holes at each end and storing them in jam jars or threaded on strings like barbaric necklaces, eventually to be broken or lost or thrown away.

There were no laws prohibiting egg-collecting. Indeed, most natural history books gave precise instructions on not only how and where to find specific nests, but how best to prepare and display the eggs. The village boys affected a kind of voluntary self-regulation whereby they took only one egg from any one nest, on the facile assumption that there was going to be more than one egg there in the first place, that "birds couldn't count", and that no one else was going to find the same nest afterwards. Nonetheless, outright cruelty was not approved of, and "the young" were sacrosanct, though often the victims of thoughtlessly too-frequent inspection.

There was one exception to these happy rulings.

The boy generally known behind his back as Nasty (there was sure to be at least one Nasty in every village, dull and backward in class and a menace to smaller children in the playground) was frequently caned by Headmaster Jones, often in front of the whole school, and held back in Standard Two under a long-suffering Bessie Bagwell while the rest of his age-group moved up to Standards Three and Four.

Nasty's springtime speciality was "strubbing" birds' nests. For dull and backward though he was in class, Nasty was as clever as anyone at finding birds' nests, which he would tear out of the hedges, smashing the eggs and pulling off the heads of any nestlings. No one could do very much about Nasty, who was big and strong for his age, almost a grown man in the eyes of the infants and the other young children.

I often wonder what became of him. Perhaps a decade or so later the war was able to make use of his ruthless and inhumane propensities, so that he spent it destroying German machine-gun nests or decapitating Japs. But somehow I doubt it. He probably escaped military service altogether on the grounds of diminished intellect.

PC Holman, bane of the youth of the village and a few of its grown-ups such as Fred Gee, thought nothing of administering instant justice if he caught boys up to mischief. Sneaking up to them unsportingly on his silent-tyred police bike as they emerged literally red-handed from a strawberry field or out through a gap in the hedge of an autumnal orchard, he would slap them about the head with his heavy police glove. But it would have been no use expecting him to waste time trying to catch Nasty red-handed at his springtime sport.

Oddly, in spite of the combined depredations of Nasty and the other boys, there was never any scarcity of wild birds in the district. Many birds that in spite of their compulsory protection are rare today were in those days quite common. Birds' nesting and egg collecting had little effect on their numbers. What has really thinned them out are the violent changes in agricultural practices and the inexorable spread of suburbia into the countryside.

As the boys grew up and became more adventurous, one or two of them, inspired by visits to the natural history department in Exeter's Royal Albert Memorial Museum, would do their birds' nesting further afield, in Stoke Woods, for instance. Much nearer Stoke Canon than Pinhoe, Stoke Woods in those days was almost unspoilt forest, hardly touched since the wholesale felling of oak trees for the roof timbers of St Peter's cathedral church a thousand years earlier.

According to the notice-cards under each rigid glass-eyed avian specimen in the museum, Stoke Woods was, or had been, the habitat of countless exotic victims of trigger-happy Victorian and Edwardian "naturalists". Rollers, Bee-Eaters, Rose-Coloured Pastors, Golden Orioles, Nutcrackers, Hawfinches, Siskins, Shrikes, Redpolls: most of them owe their present rarity to the achievements of those avid trophy-hunters. A few species survived: buzzards, kestrels, sparrow-hawks, jays, magpies, all three kinds of woodpeckers, nut-hatches, tree-creepers, and so on, or arrived to take up residence after that one-sided war had given way to the more even-handed war of 1914-18 when the "other side" fired back.

To get to Stoke Woods from Pinhoe you tramped all the way up Church Hill, egg-collecting tins part-filled with sawdust or cottonwool in a haversack along with sandwiches, an apple, a bottle of lemonade and Cherry Kearton's book on *Birds and Their Nests and How to Find Them*, past the side-turning to the church itself, up past Beacon Down House and Cheyney Gate and on to the four-lane junction at Stoke Post. There, making sure no one saw you about to trespass yet again, you climbed over a gate, hurrying down the steep slope of Drew's Clieve, like a guilt-ridden fox running from the baying of the fox-hounds at Silverton Kennels at the top of the slope, to reach cover among clumps of high yellow furze and young green bracken and finally to plunge into the depths of mixed deciduous giants and lofty conifers.

The forest floor, broken here and there into fern-fringed threads of running water, was upholstered elsewhere with great peaty mounds. A boy would find them deceptively warm and comfortable for sprawling on while sampling sandwiches and lemonade and consulting Cherry Kearton on the possibilities of the ivy-covered tree-forks overhead, until he suddenly leaped up from the shock of a thousand red-hot needle-jabs. Prancing about in agony, he would brush frantically at various parts of his anatomy to rid himself of the attacks of the advance-guard from the nest of indignantly aggressive wood-ants he had been sitting on, none of them less then half an inch long and all with bites like an electric shock.

By way of a change from the mixed allurements and perils of Stoke Woods, Stanley and Denny once wandered in a different direction along the dusty-hedged Cullumpton road, past Moonhill Copse whose lofty elms had earlier in the year preserved its clamorous colony of rooks from the boys' acquisitive attentions, past the ball-topped sentinel pillars at the wooded entrance to Poltimore Park and the abandoned sandpit and across the River Clyst at Withy Bridge.

There, they made for a clump of Scots pines high up in the middle of a field, having for no sound ornithological reasons convinced each other that it looked just the place for a raven's nest. Instead it proved to be just the place for an elderly gentleman in a knickerbocker suit who stepped out from a gateway and demanded, mildly enough, what they were doing. "Birds' nesting," they told him frankly, though inwardly uneasy about the imagined penalties, not for birds' nesting, but for trespassing. "What sort of birds' nests are you looking for?" they were asked next with an indulgent smile. Their ambitions for the morning's expedition being centred on that one particular species, and the old gentleman looking and sounding unusually friendly for a grown-up, they told him. He might even, they half hoped, be able to help them. And so he did, if only in a negative way. "No ravens around here," he told them through his great white moustache. "You boys want to try up on Dartmoor." Dartmoor to them being next door to the moon, they thanked him politely and wandered back to the road, secretly relieved not to be prosecuted (or was it executed?) for trespassing.

It was several years before they learnt who the old gentleman was: Eden Philpotts, the writer and dramatist whose home, Kerswell, was only a few hundred yards from where he had caught them, and whose novels and plays dealt largely with Dartmoor; which had perhaps coloured his recommendations of that locality as a hunting ground for ravens' nests, though in his gentlemanly way he may also have been recommending them to get off his land.

Apart from birds' nesting there were plenty of other youthful pastimes: catapults and ordinary catapult-less stone-throwing, the latter not only competitive but sometimes aimed with malice; conkers, hoops, tops and marbles, with hop-scotch, tag and skipping for the little maids. There was also the perennial footer or "vooter" which in a scarcely less primitive form survives today, though now seldom played on the public roads.

Most of these activities were seasonal, though not for the reasons that governed the taking of birds' eggs. The annual introduction of one and its abandonment in favour of the next seemed to be a matter of instinct or mutual agreement rather than because of any place in the calendar, though climatic conditions must have had a lot to do with the switch from one to another.

Hoops, great circles of rod-iron two or three feet across, which bounced and rang appealingly along frost-hard roads, were still free-running up to the late 1920s. All too frequently they were too free-running, careering off well ahead of their owners to cause inconvenience to patiently plodding cart-horses and much profanity from their drivers, not to mention the drivers of Morris Cowleys and Swifts and Fords and luxury Austins and Daimlers. Horses' legs and motorcars' front wheels could easily become trapped inside those great maverick circles of iron.

An edict eventually went forth, whether on a national level or a purely parochial one no one was quite sure though Mr Jones, a member of the Parish Council, was suspected of having something to do with it: all hoops must thenceforth be permanently linked to the hooks that their owners used for trundling the hoops, so that boys and hoops should forever be united, and the latter theoretically under control. Blacksmith Rogers in his smithy on the main road did a roaring trade for a while, closing the hooks round the hoops at threepence a time, in between shrinking iron tyres onto Wheelwright Pratt's cartwheels, mending ploughs and shoeing horses. Even then, there were one or two dedicated hoopers not above bowling their captive iron rings along at speed and then letting go the hooks, which slammed round and round on the road surface in a most gratifyingly uncontrolled manner as hoop and hook careered away into the distance, decisively defeating the object of the new regulation.

Whipping-tops, which could be whipped through the air like bullets, endangering pedestrians, traffic and cottage windows alike, were fortunately not subjected to the same sort of regulation whereby the top would have to be permanently attached to the string of its whip.

Then there was the ever-popular pastime of vooter, the juvenile version involving innumerable players, few if any spectators, and everyone his own referee and linesman. It took place in the school playground before and after lessons and at other times almost anywhere in the village. There were twenty or thirty to a side, all ages and sizes, an old bald tennis ball, an empty tin or sometimes a stone, and jackets flung down at each end of the "pitch" in lieu of goal-posts. On the way home after school the goal-posts were even more imaginary and constantly changed position as play progressed along the road, not unlike the happy-go-lucky bladder-ball games of Merrie Olde Englande. Roadside gardens were used as part of the ever-changing pitch, and traffic was a barely tolerated nuisance. Any number of participants began the game but finally were reduced to two, one or none at all, according to the proximity of each boy's home and tea-time.

Failing vooter, there was always "motor-bikes". This began with lengths of forked branches pulled out of a hedge, two or three feet long, preferably slightly curved and with twigs at appropriate places as levers for clutch and brakes. A round end of a cocoa-tin nailed to the centre for a headlamp, another to one side as the licence-holder, and there was your motor-bike ready for the road.

You grasped the ends of your rustic handlebars with both hands, held down the clutch lever with the left, made wringing movements with the other and accompanied those actions with much exaggerated elbow-flapping (the "twist-grip throttle" had by that time been invented), stood on one leg and kicked down mightily with the other (the "kick start", too, was by then in general use), rendered not wholly convincing engine noises with the aid of tongue-tip against the backs of front teeth, and off you went to school in splendid style.

How you despised the silly motor-bikeless little girls trotting schoolwards along the main road with stockingless legs in laceless boots, as you *drrr-drrred* your dental and glottal exhaust at them and galloped past! You were Frank Arthur of Exeter Speedway fame on his 1,000cc Harley Davidson "down" Exeter Dirt Track, where it was every boy's rarely-realised ambition to go.

Up in the playground, half a dozen other incipient speedway riders would be careering round and round, toe-skidding, expertly changing gear, until Miss Bagwell appeared on the steps of the school porch to ring her handbell for the line up for going into class. Handlebars would be hidden in the hedge among protective brambles and nettles, to be got out again at playtime and again at midday to take you home for dinner.

Denny's boarding-school brother presented him with a genuine tax disc to stick onto his piece of tin —

long expired, as was only to be expected, from an old 1908 Douglas he had "bought" from another boy at his school and expected his father to pay for. Freddy Causley, after his mile-long motor-bike ride up and down both sides of Sandrock Hill and then through Monkerton, turned up with a real paraffin headlamp on his handlebars, deficient only in glass and wick and paraffin. 'Arry Rogers, most envied of them all, sported a little rubber horn in the shape of a dog which tooted realistically when squeezed and with true dog-like devotion alerted its owner when Nasty stole both handlebars and horn and began *drrr-drrr-ing* his way homeward in short-lived tooting triumph.

Poor little Raymond Jewell, from Beacon Cottage opposite Beacon Down House, had no handlebars at all. He suffered from a mysterious illness that prevented him from exerting himself to the extent that most boys usually did, but he was sometimes allowed to hold someone else's handlebars when he would *drrr-drrr* delightedly to himself, without letting in the clutch.

Farther Afield

On its first appearance the Pinn Brook seeps out of the ground at a point known (somewhat whimsically) as Pinn Head, in a wooded *clieve* under Goffin's Farm, about half a mile north of Beacon Down. A hundred feet lower down it was long ago dammed up to power its one and only mill, the remains of which still stand beside the gaunt Queen Anne red-brick Pinnbrook House, built for the Whig politician Sir John Elwill at the tiny hamlet of Wuttun or Wootton. It was Mr Daniels's farmhouse in the 1930s but is now an old people's home.

Thereafter it flows, somewhat to the west of the still flourishing brick-yard, under the two roads at the Chancels and Venny bridges, then skirts the site of the former Pinhoe Tennis Club. Channelled under a little stone bridge (under two of them at the new Manor Gardens) and then humiliatingly culverted under the high M5 embankment, it meanders less restrictively, though certainly no wider under its last little bridge, the timber-railed one in Lower Langaton Lane, past the place where the sewage farm came perilously close to polluting it, and then where the minnow and water-cressed rivulet from Orman's Well once helped to purify it.

From there it carries, or used to carry, its own little shoals of minnows and sticklebacks and "millers' thumbs", further hapless victims of juvenile predatory collectors, armed with home-made nets and jam-jars, till finally it joined gentlemanly Farmer Gent's sacrosanct trout stream, not far from where the Pinhoe boys used to swim. This trout stream was an artificial "distributary" forking off from its parent River Clyst some distance upstream on the other side of the railway embankment.

In wet weather, as I have written, the river would flood, but for most of the year the part of the river where the boys did their swimming was seldom more than three or four feet deep, while upstream and down its shallows were choked with yellow-headed waterlilies, tall reeds and rushes, crow's-foot and pungent water-mint: haunts of sedge and reed warblers, moorhens, water-rails, little grebe, great dragonflies and myriads of moths and butterflies and lesser insects. Farther up still, immediately downstream of the double-arched stone bridge that carried the Waterloo line and the great King Arthur Class locomotives as well as the local puffers, lay the legendary Bottomless Pool where only the most daring or foolhardy boys and youths cared to swim.

You could clamber up the steep sides of the embankment and onto the parapet of the bridge (preferably, but not always, when no trains were to be expected) and jump the ten or fifteen feet into who knew what depths of smooth greenish water. No one ever claimed (at least not truthfully) to have touched the bottom. Certainly no boy's modest fishing-line ever plumbed it.

Today all that has changed, and changed for ever. In the late 1930s the line of the river was diverted at that point in an attempt to get the better of Nature, which succeeded only in destroying the myth of a bottomless pool as well as the advisability of jumping into it from the top of the bridge. The pool is now a good ten feet less bottomless than it was then, and an ugly jumble of rocks left over from building the bridge and formerly well beneath the surface further discourages aquatic adventures.

A safer and more popular bathing place a quarter mile downstream was not always a mere three or four feet deep. Half a mile farther down again stood Pinn Mill, properly if less commonly known as Carrow's Mill, but really Harris's Mill in Denny's young days. These days, its ivy-covered red stone ruins stand isolated and waterless except when winter floods surround it. But until the early 1930s the mill was still in use, and to give himself a working head of water Miller Harris would wind down a sluice-gate a few hundred yards up-stream to cut off the overflow into what boys called "the whirlpool" and so raise the level of the main river all the way up as far as the Bottomless Pool. At such times the village boys would arrive for their swim to find the water glittering brimful almost over the top of its banks, a truly thrilling sight in the summer sunlight.

Most of them did their bathing with nothing on, birthday suits being cheaper than the cotton variety and easier to dry. They got into the reprehensible habit of prancing about on the bank, showing what little they had to the passengers in the trains crossing Double Arched Bridge a few hundred yards upstream. One of them stood up thus in his happy state of nature one warm afternoon drinking lemonade out of a bottle and the same coloured liquid leaking out from his other end a moment later. "Cor, look — no kidleys," pointed out one of his companions, who was blessed with some rudimentary biological knowledge. Much vulgar mirth all round.

There were of course no "liddle maids" present. Few of their supposedly gentler and more refined sex ever went to the river. Little maids stayed at home with mother, as little maids always should, or they took their dolls or small brothers or sisters out in their prams up and down the shaded lanes.

For the boys, when not bathing in the River Clyst there was always "vishing". The Clyst in those days was rich in all manner of fish, from the lordly leaping grayling to the humble gudgeon, as well as minnows and sticklebacks, loaches and eels. No boy ever caught a grayling or even a trout. Roach, dace and gudgeon were the usual victims to their bread pellets and bluebottle maggots and garden worms. Some stretches of the river were leased to the Exeter Angling Club, whose members turned up complete with everything "the compleat angler" could possibly require, in impressive contrast to the hazel sticks and parcel-string and bottle-corks and bent pins favoured by the village boys.

Eels or "ails", however, were fair game for anyone. Sometimes an old fellow came out from Exeter "clatting" for them for his weekly fish-stall in Sidwell Street. For this he used an old umbrella suspended from a stick upside down and open over the water, and a bunch of dung-worms, known to him as "angle-dwitches" (perhaps because "angled" with and then "dwitched" or twitched up), each threaded through with a short length of wool or worsted and dangled (as well as angled) from the end of a line on another stick. The eels obligingly got their teeth tangled up in the wool long enough for them to be whipped, or twitched, out of the water and allowed to drop off into the inverted umbrella. Despite their eponymously slippery reputation this was of no help to them when trying to escape up the concave interior.

No boy ever tried his luck at clatting, which would have required not only possession of an umbrella but also a lot of messing about with needles and wool and equally slippery angle-dwitches. But bent pins often got swallowed so far down that the unfortunate eels had to be slit down to their vents before the precious hooks could be retrieved. By then, a fine tangle they would have made of your fishing-line!

Skinning an eel before cooking was fairly easy once its head was off. Like peeling off a wet glove or sock the skin came off in one piece, inside out.

Eels made delicious eating, their flesh surprisingly delicate and with no loose bones — though the way they wriggled about in the frying-pan minus heads and guts and skin could be a bit off-putting. Eels (or ails), it was firmly believed, never died till after sunset, no matter in how many pieces they were chopped.

Mr Fred Gent (yet another Fred!) from Moss Hayne Farm, who owned the fields on both sides of the railway line and embankment and Double Arched Bridge and downstream well beyond Carrow's Mill — in fact the whole of our favourite summertime resort lived up faithfully to his promising patronym. Whereas most farmers regarded boys wandering over their land as threats to their stock, crops, gates and hedges, and were not above blasting off charges of rabbit-shot at them to encourage them to leave, Farmer Gent was hearteningly easy-going. "I don't mind you boys swimming and fishing from my land," he told them on one occasion, "as long as you don't go trampling through my standing hay. And don't let me catch you fishing in my trout stream or there really will be trouble!"

Consequently, they always threaded their way carefully round the edges of Farmer Gent's fields of standing hay, never tried out their bent pins and garden worms on the occupants of his trout stream, despite the tempting ripples and circles on its surface, and conscientiously left his gates exactly as they found them. Elsewhere, save in the fields belonging to the no less benevolent Farmer Hodge, boys trampled down the hay, stole swedes and turnips and apples and strawberries in season (PC Holman's absence permitting), and pulled gates wide open if they found them closed and closed any they found open, so that cattle strayed out into the lanes or milled about in front of a closed gate on returning from milking. Indulgent Farmer Hodge and gentlemanly Farmer Gent never suffered from such annoyances.

Sometimes by way of a short cut to the river, especially on Sundays when there were fewer trains about, they would go down for their day's swimming or fishing along the railway line, rather than across the fields lower down, squeezing through a gap in the thorn hedge beside a tall locked wooden door not far from the sandstone bridge across Langaton Lane, and up the steep slope of the embankment onto a cindery path alongside the permanent way.

This really was trespassing (the Penalty for which, according to many a cast-iron notice-board, was at least Two Pounds — which to them might just as well have been Two Thousand). Even on a Sunday a train might still come along; and if from behind them, then the spirit of devilry got too much for the trespassers and they would compound their daring, risking thoughtless lives and parental distress by getting onto the track a quarter mile or so in front of the oncoming locomotive and clattering along on the sleepers in their loose hobnailed boots, spurred on by furious whistlings of steam till, with the monster almost on top of them, they would hurl themselves sideways and go tumbling head over heels down the embankment, the clank and racket of wheels and roaring and shrieking of the whistle all but drowning the shouts of driver and fireman leaning from their cab.

Usually the monster would be one of the local "slow" 2-4-0s (built in the late 1800s with tall flared brass-bound funnel and high protuberant dome) — small fry which would "only" have mashed them into pulp if it had caught up with them. Now and again, however, they got in front of a great King Arthur Class express just settling into its stride after leaving Exeter Queen Street station four or five miles back and already going twice the speed of the humble local.

Great was their frightened pride when they picked themselves up at the foot of the embankment and squeezed through the wire fence into the sanctuary of one of Farmer Gent's water-meadows. "Cor — that was *Zur-Lancelot!* 'Er wadn' 'arf travelling!" They would gaze after it with a sense of achievement as the irate shouts of driver and fireman faded away and the swaying black end of *Sir Lancelot*'s rearmost coach receded into the distance towards Broadclyst Station. Perhaps the river smelt, felt and tasted all the cooler and sweeter after an apparently narrow escape from a messy end.

Another, slightly less dangerous kind of railway game was to nip up the embankment to the line when a train was heard approaching in the distance and carefully place a precious farthing or an even more precious ha'penny on top of one of the rails and make oneself scarce until the train had passed over it. Sometimes, search as one might among the sleepers and greasy ballast-stones and both pairs of rails the coin would have disappeared, which was not the purpose of the exercise. But usually it was to be found lying somewhere near where it had been placed, the farthing now bright copper and wafer-thin and about the size of a ha'penny, and the ha'penny similarly about the size of a penny. This was no way to double a meagre fortune, however. The wafer-thin coin was of no use as coin of the realm, so it was not a game to be played very often, being far too expensive.

Once on one of those summery Sunday mornings, when about to slip in past the high wooden gate near the road bridge, intent on that highly prohibited and locomotive-pacing short cut, the boys heard low voices somewhere above them, and peeping up the steep slope of the embankment in authentic Red Indian fashion, as they fondly imagined, they saw three or four men in railwaymen's clothing walking slowly and purposefully alongside the permanent way. Abruptly, the boys changed their minds about their route to the river, taking the slightly longer, less dangerous though still technically trespassing route across the open fields, making a great pretence when they came in sight of those patrolling figures of not noticing them, though to their guilty minds it seemed certain *they* had noticed *them* and would have drawn the correct conclusions.

Sometimes on warm evenings after their work and on Saturdays and Sundays the young bloods from the village came roaring down to the river on their motorbikes, propping those status symbols against the wire fence in the nearby lane and, in deference to Farmer Gent's provisos, carefully skirting his standing hay, like everybody else. Invariably they made for Double Arched Bridge and the Bottomless Pool. There they would peel off their heavy clothing, their jackets and waistcoats and clumsy hobnailed boots, thick "cords" and woollen "coms" or "long johns", exchanging them for thin full-length cotton "costumes". Clutching lumps of kitchen soap, they would climb up to the parapet of the bridge and jump off, floundering about in those unknown murky depths (most of them could support themselves in the water after a fashion), and soap themselves all over, costumes included, polluting the river with soapsuds and the sweet summer air with their shouting and splashing. Then they would haul themselves out onto the bank, rinse the mud off their feet as best they could, and briskly towel themselves dry before putting their clothes on again, thick woollen

110

coms and all, and trudge back to their bikes in the lingering heat of the early evening, cleaned and brushed up, all set to pick up their birds for their evening out.

On one memorably surprising Sunday morning Mr Jones startled and disconcerted his two sons by suddenly announcing that he was coming down to the river for a swim. This was something he had never done before; nor for that matter had Howard in recent years, as far as Denny was aware. As for Denny, he was anything but pleased not to be going on his own, or rather with his usual companions. None the less, off went all three under a fine hot sunny sky, father having arranged with wife and mother to be back home by lunch-time, which itself upset Denny's usual summer Sunday midday picnic. (This was after he had left the church choir on account of a no-longer reliable treble voice, thus releasing him for these more secular diversions.)

But most disconcerting of all, when they reached the river and Mr Jones had changed into his full-length cotton costume and dived in, he took a piece of soap in with him and a scandalised younger son and a mildly amused elder one watched him turn over on his back and soap himself all over, wallowing and spluttering in a froth of soap-suds, like any village youth whose home lacked a bathroom. Perhaps Denny should have felt thankful, in retrospect, that his father and headmaster had not taken a piece of soap with him to the Reformatory School's swimming-bath.

Mr Jones never came down to the river again, greatly to Denny's relief. Perhaps he had wanted just once to recapture some aspect of his own early youth when he too had bathed (*bah*thed rather than *bay*thed) in his local river, a not-too-deep tributary of the Taff, armed with a lump of kitchen soap in the days when his family home, too, had not boasted a bathroom. For Mr Jones came of modest Glamorganshire stock, and as all true feminists insist of any man who ever marries a woman, he had "married above him". The Deeres, his wife's family, were of that enterprising clan whose name has gone down in agricultural history especially in the United States, because of the first steel plough, the first steam and motor tractors, and today's huge prairie combine harvesters.

The Gurt Vire

If only it had happened first, the Tarsprayer Fire might have provided a modest rehearsal for the real thing. For the Gurt Vire of 1925, or Great Fire of Pinhoe as it later became known, completely gutted half a dozen cottages alongside the main road and left the same number of families homeless, while its blackened and crumbling memorial remained for everyone to see and wonder at for the greater part of two subsequent decades.

Word of it travelled to school around midday by a process of rustic telegraph never properly explained. "Vire! Vire!" — The splendid news flashed around from classroom to classroom and out onto the playground. "Down on the main road. Everything's on vire!"

112

That may have been something of an exaggeration, but it in no way detracted from the excitement. It was almost the end of morning lessons, which was just as well. Every boy, and not a few of the girls, burst clattering out in their loose-fitting hobnailed boots, down past the double gates and onto the road, for once not pausing to gaze through Mrs Bindon's shop windows but cavorting and whooping with anticipatory delight towards the road in the distance, which could be seen to be blocked by unusual numbers of people and vehicles.

Something a little way past The Corner was certainly on fire. Black smoke and livid flames leapt up from the thatched roofs of the short row of cottages, where three little girls from Standards Two and Three lived but would obviously live no more. Stalwart Lifeguards from Buckingham Palace were there in force — at least, that was what they looked like to the children, in their gleaming brass helmets and dark blue uniforms and high black boots, though they must surely have needed Royal Permission to demean themselves by hauling long ladders about and much longer lengths of hose-pipe. Their two busily pumping scarlet and gold fire-engines looked regal enough for any king, and were very soon joined by a third, which arrived with its golden bell clanging.

The boys tried balancing on the thick white hoses which twisted and writhed about under their heavy boots; but they could not stay on them for very long, hardly needing to be bawled at by PC Homan to "get off them "'oses", rather like the Wolf Cubs being bawled at to "get away from them 'orses" at Beacon Down, though this time they tried to get on again as soon as "'ole 'Oman's" back was turned. At the business ends of the hoses the long copper nozzles jumped about in the firemen's grasp like narrow pouting snouts of dragons, spurting white fire and lashing about in their efforts to break free. It might really have been white fire that they were spurting, for the flames seemed to leap up higher wherever the white water reached them.

One of the ladders with a heroic axe-wielding Lifeguard high up on it caught fire. The children backed away gaping as he slid down, only just in time. They gaped at everything, uttering "Ooh" and "Cor!" and "Look at *that* — *!*" thrilled to the soul, if any of them had one. They got in everybody's way, ignoring all warnings, most of them accustomed to being shouted at by grown-ups and determined to make the most of all this fun: the roaring and leaping flames; dense black smoke; lumps of flaming and stinking thatch being dragged down with long hooked poles; frightened cottagers at tiny broken windows trying to push out such of their humble possessions as would go through. At one an earthenware "charlie" dropped out and shattered to bits at the foot of a smoking wall. There were bits of bedsteads, wash-stands, mattresses, bundles of bedding: most of it jammed in the casements and refused to be pushed out.

Yet more fire-engines came clanging onto the scene. Yet more Lifeguards jumped down, unshipped their ladders and ran out their hoses.

But then it was dinner-time and irate parents from far afield turned up on the fringes of all this activity to drag their offspring away and spoil the fun. And afterwards back to school for the afternoon, all agog with nothing but what they were missing to chatter about. But luckily they were back again shortly after four, relieved to find that the flames, though subdued, were by no means extinguished, despite the half dozen engines and hundreds of yards of pulsating snake-hoses, their coppery heads still spewing out columns of water which the lingering flames gobbled down as though asking for more.

For the three little girls who lost their homes that day the fun could not have been quite so obvious. Someone had got hold of the key to the Missionary Church by then, and such possessions as had been rescued from the flames were carried or dragged to that temporary sanctuary. Some of the newly homeless camped out there as well, among the pews and the piled up household junk, till better accommodation was found for them, for some of them at the other end of the village at Blackall Court.

Roger's, the blacksmith's forge at the far end of the row of cottages, designed to cope with fire and flames daily, was the only building to escape relatively unscathed, being provided with a tiled roof rather than a thatched one. It remained untouched, except where the fire brigade's precautionary dousing leaked through the tiles, its broad squat chimney continuing to smoke defiantly from the more legitimate but briefly neglected furnace underneath. But Blacksmith Rogers and his wife lost their cottage which was immediately next to it. The two of them, with what possessions they had rescued from next door, moved house resourcefully to the secular sanctuary of a galvanized iron shed at the rear, used normally for storing oddments of ironmongery. Rumour had it that they afterwards did their cooking and kept themselves warm by means of the same great bricked-up bellows-boosted fire that heated and softened the wherewithal for the smith's flourishing trade.

A spark from the tall funnel of a coal-burning iron-tyred traction engine must have ignited the tinder-dry thatch on one of the cottages, it was later concluded by the relevant authorities. But whatever the cause, the result lived long in the annals of village childhood recollections.

Long long after the ruins had cooled down and the last of the fire-engines had been withdrawn from the scene, the Gurt Vire was commemorated by a grave-yard of broken-down cob walls and gutted interiors under a cagework of blackened rafters. Boys wandered among the litter of rubble, to gaze speculatively up at the charred framework overhead and occasionally come upon some worthless treasure buried among the debris. An almost undamaged oleograph of the Crucifixion clung for years to the scorched and tattered remains of wallpaper on one of the few standing interior walls, which was perhaps something of a local miracle, though nobody, not even the Reverend Oliver Puckridge, made anything of it.

116

Not till after the war was the last of the rubble cleared away to make room for the garage, filling station and adjoining forecourt which occupy that position today. No motorist calling there now could imagine the drama of seven decades ago when excited cries of "Vire! Vire!" brought the children running from school towards the raging inferno. No echoes will reach them of the clanging fire-engine bells, the writhing and hissing of hoses, the angry shouts of the firemen struggling to direct them and at the same time shouting at the schoolchildren to keep away, the roaring of the fire and eruptions of burning thatch with shreds of it flying upwards on the scorched air, scared faces at tiny windows, hands desperately shoving out household treasures, and a group of heartlessly happy boys enjoying every minute of it.

The Tar-Sprayer

Following the calamitous Gurt Vire, the village made another abortive effort to consign itself to the flames, rather than suffer the indignities Fate and the Planners had in store for it, when a tar-sprayer caught fire outside the Poltimore Arms.

The tar-sprayer was an occasional visitor to Pinhoe. It appeared for work only during the hottest days of summer, as similar operations are still carried out today, for obvious reasons. Its arrival always caused great excitement among the boys.

The machine itself, superseding an earlier version that had comprised little more than a barrel of tar slung on wheels with an open fire beneath it, was only

117

slightly less prone than the previous one to catch fire.

In general appearance it resembled a crude imitation of Stephenson's *Rocket*, pictures of which every child in the school knew from "'Istry Lessons", with a tall slender black chimney like a length of cast-iron drainpipe and a coal-burning furnace under the boiler. But its wheels were ridiculously small, compared with the real *Rocket's*.

Fitted to one side was a hand-operated pump by which the molten tar could be forced through a flexible pipe to a spray-bar. This was swung over the road by one of the workmen, while others shovelled gravel over each newly tarred patch. To cool and thereby solidify the tar, the tar-sprayer was followed by a different sort of sprayer attached to a water-cart, pulled by a patient but unfortunate horse whose hooves and fetlocks soon got clogged with tar. Behind the different sort of sprayer attached to a water-cart came a group of boys who delighted in getting their boots and stockings soaking wet as well as spattered with tar. Behind the boys came a ponderous grunting and tinkling steam-roller to flatten the gravel into the tar, far slower than any railway locomotive but scarcely less fascinating in its livery of green, red and black, with huge spinning flywheel and busily agitating pistons, and just as capable of flattening any boy it caught up with.

The day the tar-sprayer caught fire was only slightly less exciting than the day of the Gurt Vire, though a great deal less drastic in its effect on half a dozen families and the appearance of the village. Flames and smoke of a most satisfying density and ferocity belched up into the blue summery sky. The roadmen desperately shovelling gravel over the machine, in their attempt to put out the flames, looked like malicious demons busily stoking the infernal conflagration rather than sweating mortals trying to put it out. The Pinhoe Fire Brigade turned up at heroic speed, helmets askew, jackets wrongly-buttoned, trundling their nineteenth-century handcart with its hose in a tangle and buckets half empty, and the nearest water the tiny ditch under the grating by the Coronation Seat, which in any case always ran dry in summer. The boys crowded round, anxious to help; they had not enjoyed themselves so much since the Gurt Vire.

But the landlord of the Poltimore Arms, fearing for his windows and the bottles of spirits in his cellars, had telephoned for the professionals. Again they came clanking and clanging out from Exeter at fifty miles an hour in their magnificent red and gold engine festooned with miles of snow-white hose all neatly coiled, and several superfluous ladders.

Nothing much remained of that reeking black caricature of a *Rocket* by the end of the day: a tangle of blackened, twisted iron in puddles of tarry water, a lingering smell of burning, and a few loitering juveniles, no end disappointed that the fun was over, with only their mothers to face when they arrived home in almost uncleanable boots and unwashable stockings.

CHAPTER
FIVE

Tradesmen

Of far more importance to the average villager than the local gentry and moneyed classes were the local tradesmen and a few enterprising itinerants from farther afield.

Among the latter was the mackerel hawker who in the height of the season came by pony-trap the seven or eight miles from the river-port of Topsham. He announced his approach with readily recognisable if almost incomprehensible cries, "Mack! Mack! Vraish macke-o-o!" getting gradually louder as he came nearer and nearer, up Pinn Lane and Station Road, with tantalising silences in between, when he pulled up at gateways and weighed out his wares. There could never have been any doubt what he was selling, though how fresh or otherwise the mackerel were after a five or six mile voyage up-river from the sea and then, after being off-loaded from boat to quayside, a seven-mile road journey in the hot morning sun without benefit of ice it is impossible to say. But I never heard of complaints from his customers. The mackerel sold for a penny or three-ha'pence each according to size, or two pence a pound.

Another tradesman who came regularly twice a week throughout the year, also from Topsham, was Edgar White, Purveyor (i.e. butcher). There was already a butcher in the village: Way, with a son at Pinhoe School and a grubby little shop on the main road just past the pub, more or less where the Chinese Takeaway stands today. In hot weather its dusty window and the hunks of beef and mutton and offal displayed behind it fairly crawled with flies and bluebottles and wasps, much to the fascination of children on their way to and from school, which perhaps explains why Edgar White, Purveyor, troubled to come all the way from Topsham, also by pony and trap. In the course of his regular trade with a more fussy clientele in and around Pinhoe over a number of years, Edgar earned a reputation for honesty and reliability as well as for the wasp-and-fly-free quality of his meat. At Westleigh, and no doubt elsewhere in the village, if no one answered the door when he called with the family joint in his wickerwork basket he would waste no time but would take the door key from its traditional hiding-place under the mat, let himself into the house, go through the hall into the kitchen, select a suitable plate from the dresser, cross the scullery, unlock the back door, go out into the tiny yard and put the plate with joint on it in the meat safe of wood-framed perforated zinc. (Refrigerators were unheard of in those days). As Edgar was paid monthly, he did not have to wait for payment, though sometimes a cheque for the previous period might be left for him on the kitchen table. He would return through the house, relocking both doors behind him and replacing the key where he had found it.

Tom Rudd, the milkman, drove a green and yellow float pulled by a lively and obliging pony, which had learnt to move on its own initiative from gate to gate. Tom would come to the door with a two-gallon can and a hook-handled dipper tinkling under the lid. Mrs Jones, or sometimes it might be Bessie, would come to the door with a jug which Tom would grasp with a grimy thumb thrust well down inside its neck. When the level of milk reached the grime on his thumbnail the jug was full.

"Thank 'ee, Mum. Marnin' Mum!" and back he went down the path while his pony moved up to Mr Finning's.

Tom had a son, Kenneth, who when he was growing up would sometimes take over the milk round. From the low steps at the back of the float he would urge the pony to unaccustomed exertions, flicking his whip past the shiny shoulders of the rattling churns as though rehearsing for the chariot race in the film *Ben Hur*, with himself in the title-role in place of Douglas Fairbanks.

Tom Rudd made his own butter and clotted cream, the left-over whey and "skimmed" being sold to Mrs Jones's prodigal poor at $1\frac{1}{2}$d. a pint. Her husband was very fond of clotted cream, a pound of it costing about 1s.6d. (about 15p). The cream was kept in a large earthenware bowl in a cool windowless room at the rear of the shop, with no hint of ice or unheard-of refrigeration, which in any case would have ruined genuine clotted. A glass dish from Westleigh was placed on the flat pan of the brass-bound scales and balanced against a suitable brass weight. The pound weight was added, and then into the dish went the clotted cream, thick, slightly lumpy, and heavy with layers of rich yellow crust.

It was Mr Rudd's daughter, Mary, who usually served the cream with a large wooden spoon to lift it out of the bowl. When the dish with the cream dropped level against the weights in the other pan, she would delicately push the residue off the spoon with her little finger to "make weight", and then equally delicately she would lick the finger with her delicate pink tongue. Denny found it fascinating to watch her doing that, as well as envying her those extra licks of cream, although presumably she need never have gone short of it.

Mrs Jones did her main shopping in Exeter, at the Devon & Somerset Stores in the High Street, whose horse-drawn delivery van came out with her previous order once a week and took away her order for the next one. But she usually called at the store when she went into town. The shop interior greeted you with a tantalising mixture of aromas, not unlike Mrs Bindon's though on a more sumptious scale. Additional aromas issued from a scarlet and gold coffee grinder and roaster, from stacks of wooden drawers high up behind the counters and gold-lettered: Cayenne, Paprika, Nutmeg, Cinnamon, Ginger, and so on, and from huge barrel-shaped cheeses draped in muslin on a marble-topped counter, where stood a solid mountain of butter, similarly covered.

The butter would be cut into and scooped out, weighed, fussed about with, patted into small brick shapes or neatly rolled, carefully impressed with the firm's D&SS trademark and finally wrapped in grease-proof paper; all by a white-aproned assistant who plainly took a pride in what he was doing. He used a pair of light rectangular wooden bats slightly smaller than ping-pong bats, known as "Scotch hands", and certainly never once touched the butter with his Devonian ones.

There was a fascinating overhead miniature cable-car system of wires, by which a customer's payment at the counter was put into a little brass pot and sent buzzing along the wires, when the assistant pulled down on an elasticated handle. Away would go the pot to a glass-fronted kiosk in the centre of the wide shop floor, where a lady cashier sat like a spider at the centre of her web. She would reach up and unclip the pot from its pulley, tip out its contents, place receipt and change, if any, inside it, hang it back on its pulley and catapult it back along the same wire. The assistant in his turn would reach up, unclip the pot and tip out its contents.

"Thank you very much, Madam. Good day, Madam."

Other shops in the city had similar systems: the ladies' department stores Waltons', Colsons' and Bobby's, and an early Woolworth's, so that a small boy's compulsory visits to such places were not without interest.

Bills and estimates were calculated down to the nearest farthing, worth consideration elsewhere than at Mrs Bindon's. Even the price of a house might be quoted as £106.15s.7$\frac{1}{4}$d. As with haberdashery and millinery shops, price-tickets might be marked 11$\frac{3}{4}$d. (under a shilling), or 19s.11$\frac{3}{4}$d. (under a pound). But larger amounts as often as not would be in guineas, which meant a shilling extra in every pound. Similar near-deceptions are practised on the shopping public today: "Only 99p", a whole one p (worth less than a 1920s varden) under a pound!

The Village Postman

The postman, a fairly frequent caller at Headmaster Jones's door on account of the latter's heavy professional correspondence, could hardly be classed as a tradesman. His name was Woodley. The Woodleys lived at Pound Cottage at The Corner, now both gone. Pound Cottage was the village post office in the early 1800s when the four or five-way turnpike was still in operation; the Exeter-Taunton mail coach went through Pinhoe, and the village pound for stray animals was close by.

Postman Woodley wore a dark blue uniform with narrow red piping down his trouser and a fore-and-aft double-peaked cap. This was also dark blue with red piping, slightly military looking, and dating from Victorian times. The cap and uniform were changed for a more up-to-date style in the late 1920s.

Later still, Postman Woodley was provided with a bicycle painted a distinctive General Post Office red, with a carrier over the front wheel for his bags of mail. Cheeky young telegram boys, in their own style of uniform and jaunty pill-box hats, cycled out from

Exeter on similarly GPO-red bicycles, but without the carriers, satchels slung from their shoulders containing presumably urgent telegrams which were hand-printed on buff forms inside orange envelopes.

William Spry, Chimney Sweep

Brought up, as were most of the children in Mr Jones's school, on the story of Tom from *The Water Babies* (before being introduced to that other Tom of Mark Twain's Mississippi tale), it was not difficult for them to see in Mr Spry with his soot-smeared features, his sooty clothes and his sooty barrow, sacks and brushes, a present-day counterpart to Charles Kingsley's Mr Grimes. He had a son, Cyril, and a daughter incongruously or defiantly named Lily, both at the village school. It could easily be imagined that Cyril, who like his father was undersized, was sent up inside the least undersized chimneys of Pinhoe's older and grander dwellings. Cyril was often to be seen on Saturdays and during the holidays accompanying his father on his rounds, when it was only natural to assume that it was one of his filial duties to perform those arduous and unenviable tasks.

The Sprys, being members of Mrs Jones's "prodigal poor" lived at the perhaps appropriately named Blackall or "Slum" Court, where its few rickety stove-pipe chimneys probably never received William Spry's professional attentions. His daughter Lily, possibly because of the saving grace of her name, showed every promise of living down her sooty heritage and growing up to be a perversely Snow Whitish young lady.

Tom Rogers, Newsagent

Tom Rogers ran a "Newsagents' and General" shabby little shop on the main road near the Mission Church, almost opposite the forge run by his brother Blacksmith Rogers and the short row of doomed cottages next to it. Tom Rogers spent most of his time behind his counter pouring over crosswords in innumerable newspapers, of which he had a free and extensive selection, while his wife Daisy and one or two of their elder offspring did the work required in his business. Tom aspired to win his fortune at the crosswords (later he added football pools to that optimistic uncertainty). As far as anyone knew he never won a penny, though he must have spent much more than that trying to.

Meanwhile, he and his wife helped swell the number of pupils at Mr Fred Jones's school, and Daisy (when able) with their daughter Charlotte and a succession of sons collected the papers from the railway station and sorted and delivered them. Now and again a son opted out for some less exacting and more rewarding occupation, but there was always another one to take his place. Dick, he of the never-completed stories on the way up Church Hill, was one of these. Another was Harry, who rode his delivery bike with great skill and panache, the give-away legend "Express & Echo" attached to its cross-bar denoting its true ownership.

Most of that family now rest at peace in the churchyard, though a younger member still runs the local stationer's and newsagent's — but at the drastically transformed Corner instead of next door to the Mission Church.

127

Itinerants

Less indispensable or more unwelcome itinerants included the knife-grinder perched high on his three-wheeled box of tricks, pedalling industriously and going nowhere, the ivory handles of Mr John Finning's dinner knives sticking out from the top and trembling like skeleton finger-bones with the agony of what was going on inside. There was a rag-and-bone man who accepted "old iron", scrap lead and brass and copper; and a gypsy woman in soiled voluminous skirts and great brass earrings, who leant sideways from the weight of a large wickerwork basket. This was crammed with rows of split-stick clothes-pegs that were jammed onto long hazel spars and looked like gigantic wooden combs, and stolen daffodils and "lucky white heather".

An organ-grinder was to be heard long before he was seen (rather like the mackerel-hawker), churning out his "Lily of Laguna", "Goodbye Dolly" and "Danny Boy" over and over again. A disreputable-looking monkey in a grubby red jacket sat perched on top of the jangling instrument, industriously searching itself for fleas and apparently provided with two tails, the second being its sagging fur-clogged chain. The organ-grinder's woman went up to the cottage doors, hopefully holding out her money-pot fixed to the end of a short stick.

Exotic visitors to local villages were the French onion boys from Brittany, who came as deck-passengers on black-hulled topsail schooners and semi-square-rigged barquentines, which were locked into the Ship Canal at Turf and then horse-towed up to the quay or the

Basin at Exeter. They brought with them strange-looking high-handlebarred bicycles fitted with single long-levered front brakes, some with solid tyres, and hung about with plaited strings of outsize onions, mauve and bronze and gold. Below decks were the vessels' main cargoes — sacks of potatoes and beans, and odoriferous loads of animal bones and hooves and horns and mouldering hides for the glue factories and tanneries that comprised the main industries in that lowermost part of the town. Downstream from Exe Bridge to beyond the Basin a blind man would have known where he was by the appalling stench. The same area today has been so smartened up with ornate up-market apartments and flats as to be totally unrecognisable as well as uninterestingly hygienic, although a single surviving chimney on the western bank of the canal still discharges the same repellent yet curiously evocative odours.

The onion boys — grown men, most of them — started their journeyings into the surrounding countryside on foot, it being impossible to mount and ride their over-burdened machines. But gradually as they progressed from door to door, and housewives — though by no means all of them — fell for their broken English and limpid looks as well as their strings of onions, they were able to get at their saddles and pedals.

Headmaster Jones, if he chanced to be at home when an onion boy called, would attempt an *entente* in his Army French. He would sign to his wife to bring a few bakestones or slices of cake. "Gateau", he would offer munificently. "Tray bon — Wee?" . . . But that would only involve him in having to purchase a string of onions which, as his wife would complain to him afterwards, "didn't keep".

Then there were pedlars, one-armed or swinging along one-legged on crutches, or sporting pink celluloid eye-patches, all looking like down-at-heel pirates trying their luck at a less bloodthirsty trade. They lugged great battered suitcases around with them, packed with all manner of tawdry treasures: bootlaces, tins of polish, collar-studs, buttons, packets of pins and needles, reels of cotton, ribbons and elastic.

Mr Jones's wife would hand them a few coppers, seldom in exchange for anything, and add her standard largesse in the form of some of yesterday's scones or bakestones in a paper bag. "Old soldiers," she would explain to her young son after they had limped gratefully away; "or some of them are."

This was during the great post-war depression when others besides genuine old soldiers were out of work and some of them trying to pass themselves off as wounded heroes of the ten-years-past conflict, while most of the younger ones secretly looked forward to full employment in the next one.

More fortunate than those incapacitated old soldiers and their jobless impersonators were the present-day not yet disillusioned Regulars. In flat cheese-cutter caps, khaki tunics, breeches and puttees, they came trotting briskly up Station Road two by two on high-stepping jingling horses as polished and shiny as conkers fresh from their velvet-lined knobbly shells. Now and again they came with a gun-carriage or an ammunition limber rattling along behind them, painted green and sparkling with steel and brass. The older men, sergeants and corporals, were veterans of the recent war and still dutifully prepared to garrison Africa and the Middle East, to safeguard us against the next one. They came from Topsham Barracks, which were just outside Exeter, not at Topsham itself.

There was not much evidence of an up-to-date Army: there were a few motorised transporters and staff-cars and tanks, but not very many. As late as 1939 the Army still accommodated itself in bell tents on its practice camps, and used mules and horses, guns on wooden-spoked wheels and wooden limbers, and wore flat cheese-cutters with brass badges and buttons that needed to be polished every day, and puttees that unwound themselves at critical moments, all left over from "1914 and all that".

Meanwhile, in his recently defeated Fatherland across the Channel, an upstart little man with a toothbrush moustache and distinctive forelock was busily building up the most modern and formidable fighting force the world had ever known.

In this country, in the neighbouring town there were armies of street-cleaners, successors to the crossing-sweepers of half a century earlier, with two-wheeled barrows and shovels and brooms to clear away the horse droppings left by the drays and delivery vans, especially from the thin, shiny flush-laid tramlines which easily clogged up. In villages like Pinhoe there were small boys who ran out with buckets and trowels and hand-brushes as soon as a horse appeared along the road, especially those well-fed Army horses, to scoop up the precious deposits for their fathers' gardens.

Mr Tom Tapley

Builder, carpenter and undertaker, Tom Tapley had his house, workshop and Chapel of Rest at the far end of Southleigh Terrace, next to the station footpath and Vinney Bridge.

A part of the premises, in front of the Chapel of Rest, was given over for the use of the Jubilee Club, a favourite resort of the more sober adult inhabitants of the village. It provided a sober environment for billiards, whist, skittles, darts, etc., all in lingering commemoration of the fiftieth year of Good Queen Victoria's golden reign, but without the alcoholic accompaniments to similar entertainment that were available at the Poltimore Arms and the nearby Heart of Oak.

Tom Tapley, like builders everywhere, contributed more than his fair share to the de-ruralisation of the village he lived in. As early as 1925, in partnership with a gentleman named Frame, he put up about a dozen semi-detached houses at the upper part of Park Lane on the northern fringe of the village and roughly parallel to Church Hill. Until then, Park Lane was an unspoilt area with only one dwelling, the imposing Petersfield House at its foot, near its junction with the main road. Beyond Park Lane was Hilly Field, a steep rolling incline rising up some 400 feet, to approximately the level of Beacon Down, with which it connected by two side-lanes.

The view from Hilly Field to the north and east reached well into Somerset, with the Wellington Monument clearly visible and the more local landmarks of Poltimore House, Killerton House and Ashclyst Forest in the foreground. Those who lived in Tom Tapley's houses in Park Lane, when they paused to look out from their rear windows, saw all that splendid panorama laid out below them. Each of the houses was offered for sale at £100, the view thrown in for free.

How anyone could build and sell a three-bedroomed dwelling-house for £100 and show a profit, even in those days, is one of the financial enigmas of the times.

That was of course before the greatest days of Trade Union interference and restriction, and Tom Tapley's work-force consisted of no more than three or four men and himself, who turned their hands to every trade required for building a house, from start to finish.

Tom would help dig the trenches for the foundations, mix the concrete (by hand), lay bricks, make and fit doors, windows and frames, floor beams, joists and rafters, put in all glass, do the roofing, slating, plumbing and plastering, install gas and electrical fittings, excavate separate cess-pits for each house, connect everything up, paint, varnish and decorate. Tom Tapley and his men did the lot.

That perhaps explains why a house could be built and sold so cheaply. Granted, a builder's labourer, even a skilled one (and they were all skilled at half a dozen more or less disparate trades) earned no more than £2 or £2.10s. a week with 10d. or a shilling deducted for insurance; and perfectly satisfied they all were with that apparently meagre wage. Quite a lot of their contemporaries were out of work. And Tom Tapley himself was equally satisfied with his meagre profits. If he made £10 on the sale of a house, he considered he had done pretty well. Even four or five pounds in the pocket after two or three months' labour, mainly outdoors in all but the very worst weather, was not to be sneezed at. What his materials cost him, bricks and sand and mortar, timber and tiles and everything else plus his weekly wage-bill of about £20, plus various incidentals, bear no comparison with today's rates of employment and wage structures. Judging by recent times, Tom Tapley ought to have gone bankrupt instead of ending up comfortably off.

Since his building in Park Lane a lot of other builders have followed in his footsteps, and Park Lane today is as unlike what it was in the 1920s as the rest of the village.

Sometimes work on one of Tom Tapley's houses would cease for a couple of hours of an afternoon when his services and those of his bricklayers-cum-carpenters-cum-plumbers were required for a different role. Changed into sober black, top hats, and black gloves, with the coffin they had lately knocked up in the workshop weighty with the inert human clay they had more recently arranged inside it, they assembled at the lych-gate outside the churchyard. Led by the Reverend Oliver Puckridge quavering to heaven his prayers for the dead and sometimes encumbered by a train of giggling choirboys, they would dutifully and as to the manner born intone the ritual hymns and responses and amens. Four of them would hoist the coffin onto their shoulders, slowly and steadily bear it to the graveside, and solemnly lower their brass-name-plated, brass-handled handiwork into its six-foot deep permanent resting-place, while Len Butt stood waiting in the background with his shovel.

Headmaster Jones, by courtesy of the Local Education Authority in Exeter, had an arrangement with Tom Tapley to supply the school with pieces of timber suitable for the simple joinery and toy manufacture that was done in carpentry class. In return, he once or twice obtained for one of his fourteen-year-old school-leavers an envied position with Tom Tapley's firm as apprentice carpenter-bricklayer-plumber-slater-coffin-maker, etc.

Denny, at the age of ten or eleven an enthusiastic yearner after anything that might float him up or down his beloved River Clyst, obtained his father's permission not only to use the school's carpentry workshop during the holidays, but to obtain from Tom Tapley a few lengths of wood to build a canoe.

Tom Tapley's men, who of course knew who he was, were cheerfully obliging. "Here you are then, son;" and they showed him a daunting selection of board in oak and elm. "Good coffin-board there — that'll keep the water out!" They also supplied him with a few lumps of the pitch used for sealing the joints in those ominous "wooden overcoats", but equally useful for sealing the joints of a home-made canoe.

It was to be a long time before Denny heard or read about "coffin ships". But in the designing, construction and use of his canoe he was perhaps lucky that this one did not end up as the other, in view of his lack of expertise and the materials he used and the fact that he was a very indifferent swimmer.

Master of Organisation

Mrs Jones was the wife of a parish councillor, church lay-reader and the village's chief charity organiser as well as school headmaster. In those days, when the concept of Social Security was not yet in its infancy, and the customary fulfiller of such parochial duties, the vicar's wife, in this instance poor deaf old Fanny, was not up to it, she often found herself undertaking unofficial Poor Relief. Scarlet fever, influenza, diptheria, "consumption" and typhoid were fairly common and frequently fatal, besides comparatively mild illnesses like whooping-cough, chicken-pox and measles, and children often fell sick. At such times Mrs Jones would spend whole afternoons in her kitchen making nourishing dainties: calves'-foot jellies, butter-cakes, egg custards and honeycomb moulds; and take them round in baskets to the stricken households.

Sometimes the "fever cart" was to be seen outside a cottage where a sick child lay. This was a cylindrical metal tank on iron wheels and was used for disinfecting and sterilising clothing. It looked not unlike the road-worker's water-cart without its sprinkler, and was drawn by an understandably dejected-looking horse, who might have to stand there all day between its iron shafts. Healthy children fresh from a history lesson about the Great Plague of London and its attendant death-carts held their breaths and ran past the fever cart at full speed, terrified of catching something dreadful from it.

Apart from her vaguely Lady Bountiful services on behalf of the juvenile invalids of the parish Mrs Jones, assisted by Mrs Stapleton the Infants's teacher, also helping on a purely voluntary basis, took over the catering on numerous occasions when her husband was organising "socials': whist drives, jumble sales and other events for one charitable purpose or another, including the dispossessed after the Gurt Vire. These always took place at the school, there being no village hall at Pinhoe.

There were also dances, usually during the long winter evenings. They were invariably billed as "Grand Dances" on home-drawn posters stuck up in local shop windows. Jimmy Wilde's Band from Exeter would come out to play for them, and quite a few "vureigners" from the city came with it.

Dances were usually held on a Friday night, in spite of the consequent strain on early-rising Saturday workers, thanks to the reverend Chairman of Managers' rigid refusal to sanction incursions past Saturday midnight into the Sabbath. And who on earth, and certainly in Exeter or Pinhoe, fancied going to a dance that would have to end at midnight? Cinderella belonged only to pantomimes and "Goodnight Sweetheart"!

For the children, preparations for these dances generated an atmosphere of vicarious excitement and anticipation. None of them would be there, but desks and forms had to be moved out from both halves of the main schoolroom and piled up in Mr Jones's classroom, the Infants' room being used for "refreshments". The knot-nobbled bare boards of the schoolroom floor were carefully swept, then liberally sprinkled with flakes of French chalk, and small boys were positively encouraged to slide up and down to work it well in for the easy gliding of the ladies's dress shoes and the gentlemen's patent leather pumps.

Compère and master of ceremonies was always Mr Jones, in blue pin-striped suit with white or red carnation button-hole. There would be at least two or three old fashioned waltzes (by Strauss and Lehar) by special request of the older dancers, including Mr Jones and his lady. Their stately gyrations would be grudgingly watched by the younger set sitting out on chairs around the walls, deprived of their fox-trots, quick-steps and tangoes and up-to-date waltzes, if only for a few minutes.

Each of the envied black-and-white dinner-jacketed members of the band, including Jimmy Wilde himself, in turn would lay aside his instrument (except pianist and drummer who merely had to get up from theirs) to pick a willing partner from among the village talent and dance her expertly around the floor. Oh, to be a dance-band musician when you grew up, and not an engine-driver after all!

Two hours or so into Saturday morning would come "Goodnight Sweetheart", and the "Last Waltz" and then the National Anthem; but "STOP!" thunders Mr Jones from the centre of the floor, and the scared band breaks off in mid-bar with a trickle of discordant half-notes. "If the incipient Bolsheviks and traitors to King and Country who have just sneaked out will come back at once, we will end this otherwise pleasant evening in a correct and seemly manner!" Grinning foolishly, the incipient Bolsheviks and traitors with their embarrassed birds would come sneaking back, and the band would strike up "God save . . ." all over again.

Before wireless had properly caught on and television was only in an experimental stage in J. L. Baird's laboratory, events like these, on whatever day or night they might be held, were well patronised.

Mr Jones was a compulsive organiser, in any case. He organised the re-housing of all seven families whose cottages had been burnt down in the Gurt Vire — that occasion of epic excitement for the juveniles of the village, but no fun at all for those whose homes had been destroyed.

The year before that he had organised a trip to the British Empire Exhibition at Wembley, when those of his pupils who were privileged to go found themselves accommodated in a converted stable-block in cubicles with partitions that did not reach the roof. It did not take the bigger boys very long to discover a group of friendly young ladies occupying the bunks on the other side. But Headmaster Jones soon organised different accommodation after he caught the bigger boys climbing over the partition.

He did *not* organise the brief visit to the village by Mr Lloyd George before the General Election of 1926, when the great man stood at a temporary rostrum in the middle of The Corner, with what little traffic there was steering carefully round him while he harangued a group of small boys, a handful of adults and a couple of dogs on the joys and advantages of a Liberal government. But Mr Jones, of the same political persuasion as his more eminent compatriot, attempted to organise what would have been a truly memorable reception in the front room of Westleigh, with platefuls of freshly made bakestones, daffodils in vases in lieu of leeks, and photographs of his Welsh relatives on the sideboard. Alas, Lloyd George was due at Sir Francis Acland's house at Killerton to address a gathering of some 19,000 of the local electorate in the park on his new Land Campaign, and the Jones family lived on bakestones amid the perfume of dying daffodils for the rest of the week.

Another time, in August 1927, again with only limited success, Mr Jones organised a dawn expedition to the top of the tower of St Michael's Church to view an eclipse of the sun. Perhaps there are some in the village who remember it, and the peculiar mousy odour from the hemlock and hogweed plants in the early morning hedges on the way up Church Hill. Every child was armed with a bit of smoked glass, and strict orders not to look at the sun except through it. But he could not organise the behaviour of the sun itself, which in the manner of that orb on such personal occasions concealed its temporary shame behind a dense bank of cloud.

He later organised, with considerable help from Sir Francis Acland (with a view, no doubt, to influencing their parents" voting), an unforgettable visit by the older schoolchildren to the Houses of Parliament when, wonder of wonders, the *King Arthur* express that was to take the little party to Waterloo pulled up at the village station to pick them up. This was an event unprecedented in the fifty-six year old history of the station, with Mr Wilkins the stationmaster and his assistant, "Porter" Parker, never so important before or since, and *King Arthur* himself steaming and straining impatiently at his brakes on the level-crossing.

Sir Francis conducted his juvenile guests on a tour of the august Seat of Democracy, following it with cakes of a Liberal saffron yellow and lemonade, sucked through straws, on the famous terrace overlooking the River. He it was, of course, rather than Mr Jones, who had arranged for the halting of *King Arthur* at Pinhoe station, to avoid a preliminary short train journey into Exeter, though the latter got most of the credit for it.

Then again Mr Jones was present at, if he did not actually organise, the laying of the foundation stone for the new University of Exeter building in what were then Hoopern Fields, by the Prince of Wales in 1927. One of his senior pupils, Postman Woodley's thirteen year old daughter Margaret, was chosen to represent "Elementary Education in Devon" and to be "presented" to the Prince and afterwards have tea with her headmaster and numerous professors and civic dignitaries at Streatham Hall, unquestionably a great honour.

As a matter of course, as one of his professional obligations, Headmaster Jones organised and largely programmed the school's annual Entertainment, held during the last days of every autumn or winter term. This came as second nature to Mr Jones, who in spite of his numerous other commitments somehow found time to take part in productions put on at the Barnfield Hall by Exeter Drama League. Every pupil, except the daftest or most unco-operative like Nasty, took part in these school entertainments, if only to pull the curtains open or closed. The Infants' classroom became a "green room" bustling with teachers and participating children and bright with colourful costumes of crimpy crêpe paper, tinselly fairy wands and heavenly stars of tinfoil. Charlie Blackmore and Albert Chamberlain (two of the bigger boys) would be trying to fit themselves into the front and rear ends of the "Wonderful Talking Horse", while diminutive gnomes and elves were being reminded of their lines by Mrs Stapleton, Miss Minnie Coles, pins between her lips, was pinning up older girls' paper skirts, and Mr Jones using his perfumed Drama League greasepaints to draw moustaches and wrinkles and add colour to already highly coloured bucolic cheeks.

142

The stage, erected by the school's carpentry class with help from Tom Tapley, who had built its several sections in the first place, completely filled Bessie Bagwell's half of the central schoolroom, with steps in the doorway at the back leading down into the green room. The heavy dividing curtains of this large main room fitted conveniently across the front of the stage without having to be altered. The lighting, before mains gas had been brought to the village, was by oil-lamps, rather dim and smoky, hung on brackets around the walls, central hanging oil-lamps being deemed unsafe in classrooms of children. For that reason, too, there were no footlights.

Other people besides the children contributed to the evening's entertainment. Young ladies, recent or not so recent school-leavers, volunteered their talents, usually as singers. There was Miss Vincent with a pleasing deep contralto. Miss Snow rendered the popular "Dashing Away With a Smoothing Iron" and "Madam Will You Walk" to much appreciative applause. Miss Matty Boon did lively recitations. Miss Margaret Edwards, of Brookfields and Palmer & Edwards, although she had never attended Pinhoe School, played Beethovan on the piano. The headmaster's pianist daughter, knowing of her school friend Margaret's intended offerings, forebore from entering into unkind comparison with her.

Mr Jones himself, perhaps surprisingly in view of his disciplinary reputation in class, sang comic songs of the music-hall Bransby Williams kind, accompanied by Bessie Bagwell on the piano. Mrs Jones, down in the audience, hoped there was nothing significant in some of the words:

> Glad-ys, my beautiful Glad —
> To think of our honeymoon
> Makes me feel sad . . .
> The chalk cliffs of Dover
> We nearly fell over —
> And now that we're married
> I do wish we had!

But head and shoulders above the lot of them was the star turn of all such evenings, provided by Mrs Stapleton's husband Leslie. Leslie Stapleton was a sergeant-instructor with the Royal Marines, stationed at Plymouth. The cyclostyled programmes produced by the headmaster billed him as "Magician and Raconteur". His tricks with playing-cards, cigarettes, and watches borrowed from members of the audience and apparently smashed before their uneasy eyes, never failed to bring the house down. His "raconteurings" were riots of innocent rustic humour. If he entertained his marines in the same way in their leisure moments he must have been highly popular. His wife was complacently and deservedly proud of him.

These school entertainments were repeated over two or three successive evenings, people travelling considerable distances to attend them. The gentry as well as the *hoi polloi*, as the headmaster's wife whimsically termed them, filled the auditorium half of the main schoolroom to overflowing, the tag end of local youths and their girls crowding in at the doorway that led to the Standards Five and Six classrooms, which were otherwise empty except for the stacked-up forms and desks.

Inconveniently close on the heels of the Entertainment, with all its preparations and rehearsals, came what was generally known as the "Kurl Pardy". This was the annual Carol Party, organised, arranged, conducted and led, needless to say, by the seemingly indefatigable Mr Jones. The carol parties were repeated over several years, until their organiser left both the school and the village.

In the main, the Party was made up of current members of the church choir, including a few of the men who in their stalls on Sundays spent much of their time prodding the boys in front of them between the shoulder-blades to discourage their smirking and fidgetting. As with the school entertainment, there would be one or two outsiders, chief among them Miss Marjorie Jones, headmaster's daughter and music student, who came along in the role of organist, the organ being the wheezy little harmonium from Mrs Stapleton's Infants' room.

To convey this instrument around the village, a specially constructed trolley had been built in the school workshop, and to push or pull this contraption with the harmonium on it and a chair for its player balanced on top, two sturdy boys were required for their brawn rather than their broken trebles. One year, Charlie Blackmore (the front of the pantomime horse) and Albert Chamberlain (its rear) were roped in for haulage duties that were not without compensation in the form of mince-pies and chocolates and glasses of ginger wine provided at almost every stop.

Mr Jones, no novice at this sort of thing, sent round notice of the impending visit by the Carol Party to all the promising households in the parish, so there should be no excuse for anyone to be out, or not to hear them. In point of fact, the gentry and well-to-do knew their duties and responsibilities and never failed in either, while the Carol Party in return gave good value for money, and for more than money. No boy, furthermore, would have dared parody the words of "When Shepherds Watched" or "Good King Wenceslas" as they did (though not too loudly) at Oliver Puckridge's Christmas services in church.

On one occasion Mr Jones's elder son Howard, an inventive and resourceful young man went to a great deal of trouble to fashion Biblical-style shepherds' crooks out of old broom-handles and lengths of bent wire from which to hang candle-lanterns, with a special acetylene bicycle-lamp to light up his sister's music. In return, Mr Howard invited himself along in the role of lighting technician, in expectation of a share of the mince pies, chocolates and wine, and to hopefully ogle the maid-servants who brought it all round.

Although the proceeds went towards Church Funds, neither the vicar nor his organist choirmaster took any part in the proceedings.

Like the annual school entertainments, the carol parties were repeated each year over two or three evenings. Lady Hull's home at Beacon Down (well worth a visit) entailed a lengthy time-consuming slog

146

(especially for Charlie Blackmore and Albert Chamberlain) with only Miss Harrison's Beacon Down Cottage, where Raymond's mother was housekeeper, and the Tolchard family next door, by way of additional carolling points. And old Oliver and his tone-deaf Fanny at the Vicarage at the far end of the side-lane leading to the church could not, diplomatically, be left out, in spite of the spartan refreshments to be expected there.

In the other direction, at the lower end of the village, Arthur Dew at Monkerton Manor could be included in the interior village circuit, and deservedly got full-value "God Rest You"'s and "Good King Wenceslas'" in part-payment for visits to the pantomime. But Colonel Hext, Colonel Chichester and Mrs Featherstone (not forgetting "her Sam") entailed a further up-hill and time-consuming journey almost halfway to Sowton and Honiton Clyst, with a lot of blankly unreceptive fields and hedges in between. Both colonels were generous with their port and sherry, though lamentably short of lemonade and ginger wine for the trebles, who much to their headmaster's barely suppressed disquiet accepted glasses of port and sherry in lieu with gratification.

The 24th of May was Empire Day, another outlet for Mr Jones's organising propensities, and an occasion which like Old Pinhoe itself is now defunct. A great part of the map of the world displayed on the classroom walls in those days was coloured red. The children turned up in their best clothes, or rigged out in supposedly colonial costume: Boy Scout hat and a cap-pistol for a Canadian Mounty, a girl draped in a shawl with an earring clipped to one nostril as the Spirit of India. The Wolf Cubs wore their green and yellow jerseys and caps and scarves, and inspired by the writings of Kipling and the Chief Scout, comprised the Spirit of Colonialism in the making.

The whole school marched round and round the flag pole in the playground, saluting the proudly waving Union Flag to patriotic tunes on the gramophones: "Rule Britannia", the National Anthem, "Jerusalem", "Land of Hope and Glory", Kipling's "Recessional". Looking back from the world of today, it is an ironical memory. But it bears thinking about. "Lest We Forget". . .

The observance of other anniversaries like Oakapple Day, Poppy Day (Raymond Jewell's father had, according to Raymond, been killed accidentally the day after Armistice Day, by a celebrating fellow-soldier firing off his rifle), Queen Alexandra's Rose Day, the King's Birthday, the Prince of Wales's Birthday, Trafalgar Day, was due not so much to the organisational skills of the headmaster as to their long-standing positions in the then well-filled patriotic calendar. Fête Day and Sale of Work Day depended largely on the enthusiasm of the children and their dedicated teachers for the output of raffia-work, cane-work, basket-work, needlework, knitting, soft toys and hard toys (the latter of wood and therefore the headmaster's department).

The annual Flower Show lay outside the scope of the village school and its headmaster although he was a member of the Royal Horticultural Society, and gardening, supervised by him with the senior boys, was carried out at school in the vegetable plot beside the playground. Its produce was wheelbarrowed round the village to be delivered to selected indigent homes.

The Flower Show was held in the Fair Field, by courtesy of its owner Mr Edwards of Brookfields, nearby. There were hoop-la, skittles, a lucky dip, a roundabout and swings, an Aunt Sally, a coconut shy, a shooting gallery, a bowling alley, a contraption for testing your strength with a heavy mallet, and the town band from far-distant Cullompton, glittering and metronoming its way, left-right-left, down Station Road and Pinn Lane and then *umpah-umpah-ing* away all afternoon in a stuffy marquee; almost everything but flowers and fruit and vegetables, as far as the children could see.

Mr Jones was certainly the instigator of the dizzy elevation of a number of his brighter pupils at the age of ten or eleven by scholarship to secondary schools at Exeter, Crediton and Ottery St Mary, having coached them beyond normal elementary school expectations, along with the thirteen and fourteen year-olds in Standards Five and Six. This was preferential treatment in marked contrast to the sort he meted out to Nasty and Fred Gee.

For some of those less well-endowed academically there was "Night School", run again, needless to say, by the headmaster. This provided a kind of "further education", which numbers of his basic school-leavers made good use of, and for which they paid sixpence a twice-weekly session.

But by 1938 it was time for Mr Jones to accept another appointment and leave Pinhoe School, taking with him an MBE "for services rendered to the community", so that it fell to someone else to do the organising of whist drives and jumble sales and dances and school entertainments and carol parties in the village, and to run the night school, if any.

"Other Voke" and "Progress"

At around twenty-five to nine on weekday mornings Station Road and Causey Lane, which converged at the bottom of the lane, fairly teemed with people, mainly men, hurrying to catch the 8.40 stopping-train to Exeter Queen Street station. These were mostly shop and office workers with jobs in the city, plus a few groups of secondary-school boys and girls, all of whom would have been woken up by the seven o'clock brickyard hooter, to obey its summons in more leisurely fashion than the local workers in nursery and farmyard and at the brickyard itself.

There was Mr Crook, more honestly employed at the GPO than his surname suggests, Mr Havill (master butcher), Mr Copp from Fairview Terrace (office clerk), Mr O'Conner (fire extinguisher sales representative), and young Leonard Trelease (Lloyds Bank), who had already earned the contempt of Howard (and later somewhat imitatively his young

150

brother's) for neither smoking nor drinking, always passing his school exams, politely raising his bowler hat to almost everyone, especially the ladies, and conscientiously looking after his widowed mother and accompanying her to church on Sundays.

There were Mr Pleece, Mr Ford and Mr Lamacraft, two adventurous-minded Jacks, and Norman the brother of one of them, the distinctly unadventurous Charlie Goldsmith (ladies' hairdresser), Mr Edwards of Palmer & Edwards from Brookfield in Pinn Lane, who travelled First Class, and many others. There was a slightly sinister Mr Barnes, very friendly towards children, lisping through thick lips and offering round a bag of sweets. Boys were warned by their parents never to get into a compartment alone with Mr Barnes, though there would have been little likelihood of doing that, the train being fairly crowded by the time it reached Pinhoe Station.

Among the younger generation, mostly at secondary schools, were Joe and Leo Crook, Hedley Baker and "Farmer" Ackland (clearly unrelated to the then MP for the Tiverton Division because of the different spelling) all from Playmoor Villas, shy Gilbert Harris, middle brother of Frank and Joe, attending Technical College, sundry young ladies in blue skirts and blue-and-white gym-slips and wide-brimmed hats who were following Marjorie's, Margaret's, Mary's, Doreen's and Damaris's attendance at St Hilda's, and others at Bishop Blackall's and the Maynard School.

There was a giggling bunch of nymphs from Honiton, fifteen miles up the line; among them Muriel Hellier (Hellier's Garage) and Betty Warren (Warrens'

Bakers & Confectioners in the 1990s having a branch at Exeter, Mr Edwards's Palmer & Edwards being no more). They leant out of their carriage window as the train drew into the platform to exchange insults with the Pinhoe boys. Thankful to welcome the latter into his compartment was Edmund Gibbins from Feniton, farmer's son, after single-handedly holding the fort against feminine intrusion since boarding the train at Sidmouth Junction.

Devon General omnibuses, solid-tyred and at first with slatted wooden seats, had long been running between Cullompton and Exeter, stopping at numerous pick-up points *en route*, including The Corner at Pinhoe. By the mid-1920s the buses were still not heavily patronised, there being no shelters for passengers waiting in bad weather, while the train was not subject to so many intermediate stops.

Not until the sad day when the railways were nationalised and the railwaymen lost their company pride and sense of identity (though steam held the allegiance of some of them until that, too, was done away with), did the railways decline and the bus company really come into its own.

More recent attempts by BR or its sadly disintegrating successors to claw back something of the former company pride and with it something of its financial viability seem doomed to failure. Take, for instance, the hamlet halfway along the B3185 east of the Double Arched Bridge, still known as Broad Clyst Station.(Why it was called that is by no means obvious, seeing that the main London line from Exeter, through

Pinhoe and then over the River Clyst by that same bridge does not pass particularly near the village of Broad Clyst but rather nearer Honiton Clyst.) In the early half of the twentieth century Broad Clyst Station was on the London & South Western — later Southern — line to Waterloo, with its own goods yard and sidings and regular clientele of passengers. Where the latter came from is not obvious, although as an operating station it soon generated a cluster of dependent habitations and ancillaries including a pub.

At the end of the century the line itself, despite having been down-graded to a dangerous-looking single track in accordance with post-Beeching and post-company economics, appears almost as busy as ever. But it has the obvious limitations of a single track and no longer provides the thrilling sight of two steam trains passing each other at speed from opposite directions, instead being used by pathetically headless, tailless (or are they amphisboenic?) and nameless, characterless diesel zombies that hurtle along it. All three stations and quite as many halts between Exeter and the next double-tracked passing-place at Honiton Town are deserted ruins, left over from the golden age of steam and company pride.

Now, at the former Broad Clyst Station, an out-of-town retail store has sprung up on the site of the railway buildings. There is every certainty, too, that further desecration of the countryside around poor old Pinhoe is in the pipe-line, in addition to the completion of such controversial works as the "dualing" or re-routing of the nearby A30, which skirts what used to be Causley's Market Garden and the now even more vulnerable acres of the former Red Hayes estate.

Most children from Pinhoe school, from the year it was built, in 1887 according to the sandstone figures over its portals, to the end of the 1930s, were fated to be affected by one, if not both, of the twentieth century's World Wars. The Crimean and Boer Wars, comparatively minor affairs, had made few demands of the kind that later were to destroy so many lives and families.

There seemed to be few reminders of the South Africa idiocy in the village, though the earlier one was commemorated by Plevna House and Alma Cottage, the latter demolished in the course of Pinhoe's lemming-like rush towards its own loss of identity. And there used to be an old fellow who sat in the sun on the Coronation Seat at The Corner, watching the world of those late inter-war years go by, sucking at his clay pipe and spitting into the ditch where it emerged from beneath the hedge behind him: he was rumoured to be a veteran of Inkerman.

The granite Memorial up in Pinhoe's churchyard gives adequate proof of the village's contribution to the two World Wars, though perhaps contribution is not quite the right word. Few potential war heroes marched or sailed off to battle with the intention of being heroes, certainly not dead ones. War was a gamble in which they became the hapless stakes. Many of them took heroic risks and lost out, others were

154

forced to certain death with the alternative of being shot for cowardice. But few, if any, deliberately "gave their lives" as so many post-war eulogies, including the one on this Memorial seem to imply. The crude truth is

> They did not give their lives;
> They had them taken
> From them,
> Rudely and hideously and wastefully.
> Those that think otherwise
> Are sadly mistaken.

From Pinhoe there were twenty-five of them between 1914 and 1918 but, mercifully, fewer in 1939-45; these included Sergeant Maurice Causley, younger brother of Freddy of the market garden on the London Road side of Sandrock Hill, expert stone-kicker and birds' nester and long-distance catapulter. There is a snapshot of young Maurice Causley taken in 1923 at a school fête in the grounds of Mrs Livesey's Broadparks, one of the sixteen in the front row of the assembled school. He looks a little thoughtful and forlorn, as though even then, at the age of five or six, he has a feeling he has only another eighteen years to live.

Poor Raymond Jewell, in the second row of that same photo, has less than that, but not because of the war. Raymond's war-widowed mother was housekeeper to Miss Harrison of Beacon Hill Cottage, almost opposite Lady Hull's Beacon Down House. Raymond, suffering from his mysterious sickness, although of an age with Stanley and Denny and Freddy and many others, was never able to take part in their more strenuous activities. Instead he became a kind of protégé of the Tolchard brothers, Maurice and Albert (he of the grave-exploration episode), whose father was Miss Harrison's chauffeur and lived in the adjoining Laurel Cottage. These two boys had appointed themselves Raymond's protectors, apparently dedicated to shielding him from the usual rough and tumble of playground life. They were both older than Raymond. Pick a quarrel with him and you automatically picked a quarrel with Maurice and Albert and soon got your eye blacked by one or the other of them, sometimes both. Raymond was one of those selected by his headmaster for an educational future extending beyond the school leaving age of fourteen. He left Pinhoe School at the age of eleven with a scholarship to King's School, Ottery St Mary.

But Raymond did not stay there very long. He succumbed to his illness ten years before the war, and lies buried in a corner of Pinhoe's St Michael's churchyard. "Raymond Hope Jewell, 1916-'29". In Standard Six he sat among the thirteen and fourteen-year-olds, where Headmaster Jones good naturedly but with unconscious irony used to call him his "precious little ray of hope". The fruits the gods love best they gather first.

Some time in 1927 a brief news item appeared in the *Devon & Exeter Gazette*, reporting the mysterious disappearance in the South American jungle of

Colonel Fawcett the explorer. Lieutenant-Colonel Percy Harrison Fawcett, DSO, FRGS, soldier, surveyor, artist and cricketer, was also the inventor of the "ichthoid curve" that revolutionised the design of racing-yachts. At the time of his disappearance he had gone in search of the fabled city of Eldorado, leaving home, wife and younger son at Stoke Canon, near Pinhoe.

Inspired by this news, three young would-be adventurers from Pinhoe, Jack Lamacraft (Stanley's older brother), and Jack and Norman London, concocted a plan to go to South America in search of the missing explorer. All three were former pupils of Pinhoe School and more recently of Heles', Exeter, and all were already heroes in the eyes of the younger Pinhoe boys because of their expertise at fishing and shooting and similar manly accomplishments.

Nothing much came of the idea, as was only to be expected. But the whole of the British Empire rather than just the Brazilian jungle was open to adventurous young men in those days. Jack Lamacraft went to Canada to join the Mounties, which did his reputation among the youth of the village no harm at all, Jack London sailed to New Zealand to shoot deer and rear sheep, and his brother Norman, only slightly less adventurously stayed at home, and in emulation of Henry Bindon and Freddy Patch, started a garage and filling station on the aptly named London Road, near Honiton Clyst. It is still there today under different ownership, like a second one that Norman opened later on the Exmouth road.

Nothing more has been heard of Colonel Fawcett, (although the Pinhoe trio can hardly be blamed for that), nor his elder son (another Jack) and the third member of the little party, Raleigh Rimmel (how evocatively Devonian that first name!) in spite of several expeditions sent in search of them. One of these was joined by, and later turned into a book by, Peter Fleming, brother of the creator of James Bond. Fawcett's story was also written up by his younger son Brian. A recent attempt by an American amateur exploration party to investigate the disappearance ended ignominiously when the local Kalapalo Indians appropriated their equipment and sent them packing, fortunate not to lose their heads. The seventy year-old mystery is not likely to be solved now.

Modest local adventures came almost every child's way, though there were never any mysterious disappearances or sordid tragedies and no suspect perverts, apart possibly from Mr Barnes.

There was no school transport in those days either, and no need for it for a school that dealt with all local children from the ages of five to fourteen.

Some of them travelled quite long distances, usually on foot, bicycles being hard to come by, though now and again a boy or a girl would turn up proudly on a cranky old machine with rusty mudguards, frayed tyres and a chain that kept coming off. In the course of their journeys, achieved as a rule at a kind of "Scouts' pace", alternately walking and running, a whole day's worth of diversions might be crammed into the half hour or so it took to cover the distance to school.

The Tolchard brothers and their protégé Raymond Jewell had both ways of a mile-long hill to go, when they were sometimes flattened into the hedge by a herd of droving cattle or had to nip smartly over a gate to escape from Gypsy Penfold's stud stallion, broken loose and rampaging after a mare. At other times they met the Silverton Hunt jostling forth from the kennels in immaculate "pink" off-set with black and white in the morning, or dragging homewards, mud-and-blood spattered, in late afternoon. Miss Barbara and her mother would go by, all but unrecognisable in tight hunting fig on their high-stepping chestnuts, Lady Hull top-hatted, long-skirted and riding side-saddle. The three Wolf Cubs, out of uniform and caught waist-deep in a pack of milling fox-hounds, would straighten up and salute respectfully, just the same.

Tom Eveleigh came from Honiton Clyst, beyond the other extreme of the village. It was a good mile outside the catchment area for Mr Jones's school but he was sent there by special arrangement with the authorities, at the request of the headmistress at Honiton Clyst, who had found herself unable to cope with the excesses of that nine-year-old would-be stand-in for Nasty and Fred Gee. Tom did his best to compensate for Mr Jones's corrective treatment by leading Denny astray, instructing him in the art of poaching as practised by gypsies and Oliver Jennings, and how to haul dace and roach and the occasional trout out of the River Clyst on the Sowton estate without net or hook or the blessing of the landowner, Colonel Garret.

159

The Causley brothers probably had the best of the fun, catapulting their way mainly backwards up and down Sandrock Hill, the mile or so from their father's market garden on the Honiton road, as though the recoil from hazel-stick Y-forks and strips of lorry-tyre inner tube were their main means of propulsion. They were always the first to report the arrival of sand martins at the Rock and even more exotic birds on the Sowton Marshes. In autumn they brought huge bundles of wild flowers and berries to school for Miss Bagwell's drawing and painting lessons, and on Oakapple Day enough of those historic emblems to supply everyone with the time-honoured button-hole. They frequently quarrelled bloodily with each other, in school and out, but if one of their number was threatened by an outsider they immediately united against the intruder.

There was a murky pond of anecdotal depth in an abandoned quarry halfway down Sandrock Hill, where the Causleys kept for navigational use a flotilla of rusted-through tin baths and wash-tubs, patched up with rags and mud. That neither brother drowned was thanks to quick fraternal action with lengths of tree-branch, though wet-through clothing sometimes caused discomfort at school and must have taken a bit of explaining in the evenings, when capsizes occurred on the way home.

From the opposite direction came a second Raymond and his sister Ruby, all the way from Goffin's Farm on the 400-foot ridge overhanging the uncertain source of the Pinn Brook. This was well on the way to Stoke Canon and only just inside the Pinhoe School catchment boundary, and easily out-distanced the more modest mile-long journeyings of the two Tolchard brothers and the other Raymond, whom brother and sister caught up with or left behind on mornings or afternoons.

Another boy, George Marks, came from West Clyst Cottage, opposite the rook-haunted Moon Hill Copse halfway to Poltimore, along a not very interesting dusty-hedged main road. There was yet another George from the lodge at Red Hayes, who as often as not had to run the gauntlet of the Causleys' line of catapult fire at the Sand Rock turning.

These long-distance pupils brought their dinners with them (there were no school dinners then, any more than there was school transport). In fine weather they ate them out of doors in the playground. Otherwise, they clustered round a couple of coal fires behind high iron-rodded guards, one at each end of the main schoolroom, the girls decorously gossiping at one end, the boys squabbling and larking about at the other, flinging insults at their feminine counterparts and trying to swap their "trickle sangwidges" and lumps of lardy cake for a couple of the Causleys' hot-house tomatoes.

Of the teachers, only Mr Jones went home to dinner. The others brought sandwiches and thermoses and ate together in the privacy of Mrs Stapleton's classroom, where their proximity helped keep order next door. All three ladies came to school by push-bike, rain or fine. Mrs Stapleton, from Summer Lane at Whipton, had little to go home for at dinner time, having no children and her husband being with his Marines at Plymouth. Miss Minnie Coles lived with her two sisters and their mother at Wootton, or "Wuttun", at the far end of lonely Harrington Lane in one of four cottages opposite Pinnbrook House, which at that time was occupied by Farmer Daniels. And Miss Bessie Bagwell cycled all the way from Budlake near Killerton, on the Acland estate.

All too often some of the long-distance children, especially the boys, would have eaten most of their dinner during the mid-morning playtime so that at the proper dinner hour, with appetites already cloyed after too much thick white bread spread thinly with margarine or black treacle and hunks of heavy cake, they would cheerfully chuck what was left of it at each other out in the playground. Even apples, relatively hard to come by during the middle part of the year so that anyone eating one would find himself being earnestly begged for its core, at times of plenty in autumn would be used as missiles.

"It's always the poor who throw away most," was one of the headmaster's wife's most frequent expressions of disapproval; "which is why they remain poor." In the Jones household nothing edible was ever thrown away, except to the robins and blue-tits in the back garden. Stale bread to which was added butter, milk, sugar, sultanas and spices (which perhaps the poor could not afford) went into appetising bread-and-butter puddings. There was never any question of wasting her cakes and bakestones.

Almost everybody in the school above a certain age, especially those at the noisy end of the central room at dinner times, fell in love with Ruby, the little girl from distant Goffin's Farm, demurely eating her sandwiches at the quiet end. But Ruby was destined for a happier future than that of immature village Juliet, and she and her brother soon left for schools at Exeter.

POSTSCRIPT

All that was before Pinhoe's Elementary School was up-dated, enlarged and moved. Unlike the school, Mrs Bindon's curiously redolent little general shop and her husband's inodorous coal office and weighbridge next to it are not now anywhere in the village. Henry Bindon's garage and filling station have given place to successions of similar but less profitable enterprises, all on the original site. His hand-operated Pratt's Ethyl pump would be a novel attraction there today.

Freddy Pyle's Corner Stores has been replaced by a plethora of retail shops round what was once that peaceful five cross-wayed Corner. It is quite a busy spot now, the former Corner. Not only would the old gaffers be lost without their Coronation Seat, but there is no ditch for them to spit in, though there would be far more for them to look at and spit about. There is a light-weight replica seat on the site of the Woodleys' Pound Cottage opposite, but only their ghosts sit there. If he stood in the middle of the road, trying to regulate today's murderous traffic, Charlie Cotton would not last five minutes, even with a protective shield of young hangers-on gathered round him waiting for his dog-ends.

Although all such a long time ago, perhaps Henry Bindon and Freddy Pyle between them, abetted a little later by Henry's presumptuous competitor, Freddy Patch, launched Pinhoe on its slide from lingering rusticity. Despite the devastation wrought on Exeter during the war, its population did not decrease, but perversely the opposite. And as an ever-rapacious octopus of a neighbour, the city wasted no time in resuming its interrupted pre-war policy of probing farther and farther into the surrounding countryside with tentacles of concrete and brick and slate and glass.

The fanciful green-and-white city-boundary sign on one side of Pinn Hill, facing traffic from the Broadclyst and Poltimore direction and claiming a very post-war and post-natal "twinning" with Bad Homberg, says more than enough. A rather less brash city sign on the uphill slope of Sandrock Hill, just past the site of the Causleys' former home and market garden (now a "Business Park"), and a third one, signposting the motorway span across Langaton Lane, beside Robin's now well hidden Hideout, emphasise the sad reality.

Pinnoc, Penha, Pinnoo, Pinhow, Pinhoe,
it makes little difference now.
Once past those signs, consider yourself to be in Exeter.

ISIS publish a wide range of books in large print, from fiction to biography. Any suggestions for books you would like to see in large print or audio are always welcome. Please send to the Editorial Department at:

ISIS Publishing Ltd.
7 Centremead
Osney Mead
Oxford OX2 0ES
(01865) 250 333

A full list of titles is available free of charge from:
Ulverscroft Large Print Books

(UK)
The Green
Bradgate Road, Anstey
Leicester LE7 7FU
Tel: (0116) 236 4325

(Australia)
P.O Box 953
Crows Nest
NSW 1585
Tel: (02) 9436 2622

(USA)
1881 Ridge Road
P.O Box 1230, West Seneca,
N.Y. 14224-1230
Tel: (716) 674 4270

(Canada)
P.O Box 80038
Burlington
Ontario L7L 6B1
Tel: (905) 637 8734

(New Zealand)
P.O Box 456
Feilding
Tel: (06) 323 6828

Details of **ISIS** complete and unabridged audio books are also available from these offices. Alternatively, contact your local library for details of their collection of **ISIS** large print and unabridged audio books.